a good
HOME

a good HOME

A MEMOIR

CYNTHIA REYES

Toronto and New York
www.bpsbooks.com

Published in 2013 by
BPS Books
Toronto and New York
www.bpsbooks.com
A division of Bastian Publishing Services Ltd.

ISBN 978-1-927483-48-0

Cataloguing-in-Publication Data available from Library and Archives Canada.

Cover photo: Hamlin Grange
Cover design: Daniel Crack, Kinetics Design
Text design and typesetting: Kinetics Design, kdbooks.ca

To my family,
past, present and future,
and to the stranger
who led my great-grandmother
across the river

Contents

A House Imagined

The fire glows brightly, the wood floors nearby reflecting its warmth. The burning logs smell of maple and apple wood. Embers spark. Wood ash sifts through the grate.

It's a quiet evening in our old farmhouse northeast of Toronto.

It should be dark outside, but it isn't. A thick blanket of white covers the ground, lighting up the garden. High above it, the snow traces the bare limbs of the old apple trees and tops the thick branches of the evergreen spruce. Everything is tranquil, motionless.

The photos on the fireplace mantel, taken several years before, show our mothers and daughters. Smiling, laughing, playing together. Images of happy times, family, love.

The shelves nearby house books, precious books. A copy of *The Secret Garden*, the inside page containing a few handwritten words to our younger daughter, Lauren, from her sister Nikisha. An old book of poetry that's been thumbed through at least a hundred times. The large burgundy-covered family Bible, thumbed through less often, mostly in times of leisure or times of trouble. A photo album containing scenes from Nikisha and Tim's wedding day. A book about Jamaican culture, along with one on Canadian history.

My husband, Hamlin, lies sprawled on the sofa, his face hidden behind the science-fiction book he is reading. At just under six feet tall, he has to bend his legs to fit.

A dog is curled up by his feet. Lauren's puppy, here for a visit. Julius Caesar, the tiny part-Pug, part-Chihuahua, the little brown dog with the big name. He opens one eye suddenly, making sure we haven't sneaked out of the room. Satisfied, he closes it again. In a short while, he's snoring.

"Hard to believe a little thing like this can make such a big sound," Hamlin says, laughing.

We've been in the farmhouse now for five years.

When we first put in our offer to buy the house, in the winter of 2004, I imagined Christmas lights strung through the branches of the tall blue-green spruce trees at the far end of the large back lawn.

I imagined the family dinners, the birthday parties, the beautiful gardens visible from every window, the warm glow of Christmas in every room.

Our daughters called it a Christmas house and were already planning the decorations. Hamlin – determined that this would be our last move as a family – called it our forever house. I called it our grown-up house because of its elegant, traditional rooms.

"When we move into the new house ..." we'd say as we packed boxes and crates with items from the kitchen, bedroom, and dining room of our former house.

"When we move into the new house ..." we'd say as we put off hosting dinners with friends.

"When we move into the new house ..." we'd say as we decided which items of furniture would fit nicely where we were going and which had run their course.

Then, just two weeks before the move, on a mild evening in June, another car crashed into mine.

Much later, I would look back and say: "A thing that's going to change a person's whole life shouldn't be so quick. It should take more than an instant." But that's all it took.

Injured from head to toe, on many days I couldn't walk, talk, or even think. The move into our new home barely registered in my mind. The tall maple staircase, a welcoming feature of the house when we first saw it, was now an obstacle.

The family dinners and parties, the gardening, stringing Christmas lights in the welcoming arms of the spruce trees – none of that took place.

The active, happy times with my husband and daughters did not take place.

Overnight, my life changed so drastically I could neither believe nor accept it.

On days when I descended the stairs but couldn't climb back up, I stared balefully at them, and at the house around me, giving in to a helpless feeling or two, giving voice to a swear word or three.

I was trapped. Trapped inside an old house whose thick walls blocked out all sounds, creating an unbearably pure silence. The house's spacious, high-ceilinged, traditional rooms, beautiful and grand when I had first seen them, now intimidated me as my independence diminished.

"What happens to a gardener who can no longer garden? A public speaker who no longer speaks? A writer who no longer writes? A mother who no longer mothers?" I asked my husband on one of those dark days of fury. "Am I still a gardener? Am I still a writer, a public speaker? Am I still a mother?"

I stopped there, not voicing the question I was too afraid to ask him: "Am I still a wife?"

Alone by myself one day, lying in bed, I faced the silent, empty house and asked those questions, all of them this time. The walls stared back.

Before the accident, I had enjoyed a busy, award-winning career. In my spare time, or while travelling to foreign destinations, I had also written more than fifty stories, getting some of them published, filing and forgetting most of them, moving them from house to house along with the furniture. I couldn't remember them all, but I knew that many were about the unusual homes in which our family lived, the people we met, our unexpected adventures. Some were even about my childhood home.

"We need to find them, Cynthia," Hamlin said one day, as he walked into the bedroom. He sat at the edge of the bed and patted my injured leg through the bedspread. "We need to find your stories. Can you remember where we might have put them?"

I stared at him. Remember where we had put them? I couldn't even remember what day it was. But he was determined to find them.

Perhaps in these stories, he thought, I'd be reminded of the woman I was. And perhaps this discovery would help me find the strength and faith I would need to face the uncertain future. This I saw in his eyes, the way some couples do, even before he said the words.

For minutes here, an hour there, Hamlin searched.

Over the course of nearly one year, he found the stories in old computers, ragged boxes, and envelopes, and even faded and torn plastic bags. Some were typed on pages that had yellowed with age, with the paper clips now rusted and crumbling. Some were handwritten.

One by one, Hamlin handed the stories to me, as though presenting me with precious jewels. Each time, he gave me a long look, saying very little other than, "Here's another. You must read this."

I started to read. In the pages in front of me, a new world opened up. An old world came to life.

Part One

Island Home

I say Mother.
And my thoughts
are of you, oh House.

~ Oscar Milosz

Chapter One

The Little Pink House

After a heavy rainfall, the stream that ran through the grounds of my childhood home, in the countryside of west-central Jamaica, turned into a swift-moving river. To my two older sisters, Yvonne and Pat, and me, that made it all the more appealing.

"Bet you can't go through the culvert!" one of my sisters would call out when the stream finally settled down but the water level was still high. What this really meant was: "I dare you to wade through the stream where it flows through the culvert under the road. I dare you to get to the other side without drowning."

The thing is, none of us could swim. You'd think that would have made us think twice. But we were daredevils, three girls ages six to twelve for whom resisting a dare was an admission of cowardice.

"You go first," said Pat to me one lazy afternoon.

We were standing at the stream bank watching the heavy water flow into the dark concrete tunnel. She poked me with her elbow, pushing me toward the entrance.

I had never dared to go through the culvert when the water was so high. I also didn't understand why I had to go first. But at only six years of age, I was three years younger than Pat and six years younger than Yvonne and anxious to earn their respect.

I walked along the bank of the stream and stopped. When I reached out my hand, my fingers almost touched the mouth of the culvert. From that safe distance, I peered into the tunnel. All I could see was dark water. High, dark water. It looked and smelled very different from water that flowed in the sunlight.

A lot was riding on my decision, and I knew it. Despite being only inches taller than the water level, I took a first tentative step, holding on to the side of the culvert wall. Then, after finding my balance in the moving water, I took a second step. Then the next.

My foot slipped, and I staggered. My fingers lost touch of the wall. I felt the cold, heavy water around my neck.

Heart racing, mouth clamped shut just above water level, hands thrashing, I found the wall with my right hand at the same time that my feet found their balance on the concrete floor. Then, taking a deep breath, I walked slowly, slowly, so my feet wouldn't slip again.

To reduce the terror, I closed my eyes, opening them again quickly when a truck rumbled over the road above. Daylight, at the other end of the culvert, still seemed miles away.

At last, a lifetime later, I was out of the water, safely in the sunshine. Heart still pounding, my whole body wet and shaking, I turned to face my sisters, certain they would be impressed by my great feat.

They weren't. They had been right behind me all along, ready to save me from drowning.

My first time through the culvert had been as much a test for them as for me, but neither of them ever said so. We were doing a bad thing by disobeying our mother's order to stay away from the stream on days like this one, but they were the older children and that made them responsible for my survival. This journey had been all about survival.

~

When you're little, everything looks big.

The home of my early childhood, in the late 1950s, was a one-storey house painted light pink, with a tin roof and green trim at windows and doors. A wide stream flowed at the side of our land, and there were too many trees to count.

Our house had four small rooms: a front room, a dining room, and two bedrooms, one for the four girls – Yvonne, Pat, me, and our youngest sister, Jackie – the other for our mother and father and our brand-new baby brother, Michael.

A passerby might have wondered how a house that small could comfortably hold a family of our size, especially when one room, the front room, was used for our father's business. Both of our parents worked at home, our mother as a dressmaker, our father as a barber.

But to my six-year-old eyes and mind, it was a huge house. It gave us a place to eat, listen to stories, play tricks on one another, plot the next day's mischief, go to sleep.

Our family belonged to this house and it to us as though we were extensions of each other. Not once had it ever even occurred to me that we would live anywhere else but here. Or sleep anywhere else but in the beds we children shared at night. Or eat at any other table than the one where we tucked into the food on our plates half a second after one of our parents had finished saying grace.

"Look over there!" one of the older girls would whisper loudly during dinner, elbowing the smaller child seated beside her. "Over there!"

As all heads swivelled to look at a faraway spot, a quick fork speared a small dumpling on someone else's plate. The dumpling found its way into a mouth, and was swallowed almost immediately. When the family's eyes turned back, the culprit sat with an innocent look on her face, while a younger child stared at her plate. Maybe she'd made a mistake. Maybe, just a moment ago, only one dumpling sat on her plate, not two.

The house never seemed crowded, even when our cousins came for summer holidays. We spent almost the entire day playing on the acres of land around our house. We ran barefoot through the fields, climbed the trees, and waded noisily across the wide, sometimes muddy stream that flowed, flooded, and sometimes only trickled, through our property.

The sounds of home and family were everywhere: children yelling and laughing, water splashing, the anxious call of our mother when we climbed too high up a tree or wandered too far away in the stream.

The trees were tall, but my sisters, cousins, and I were monkeys, scampering easily up their trunks and branches to pick fruit, or just to prove that we could. That any tree should think itself beyond our reach – the very thought insulted our pride.

If a tree trunk was too thick for us to climb from ground level, we simply climbed the smaller tree next to it, then swung to the large one, yelling and squealing as we let go of one branch and fiercely grabbed the other, pretending to be Tarzan. Then we continued climbing to the very top of the big tree, competing to see who could get there first, yelling triumphantly once at the top.

Danger was all around us, but it didn't usually scare us. With loving mother, father, and siblings nearby, with our perfect house, wide stream, and many trees, we felt perfectly safe.

Mama had five rules for her own children and those visiting.

Number One:	Stay away from the stream during and after a rainfall.
Number Two:	When you leave the house, always wear clean underwear.
Number Three:	Do not steal the neighbours' fruit.
Number Four:	Always mind your manners.
Number Five:	Always stay together, no matter what.

We – especially my older sisters and cousins – tried to obey those rules. But as we tore through our breakfast, eager to start the day's adventures, we remembered only the last two: we minded our manners every time we came across an adult, and we always travelled in a pack.

We had a small farm with goats, chickens, and sometimes pigs. The children's job each morning was to lead the goats across the road to the grassy pasture facing our house and tie their long ropes to the trees there. Only then could we visit our friends. Every morning, we crossed the road together, goats trailing behind or alongside us.

We knew all the neighbours, and they knew all of us. We slipped through fences to play in their fields, climb their trees, and break yet another of our mother's rules, picking and eating their fruit as if it were our own. Only one neighbour was offended. Unfortunately, she owned the tree that bore the sweetest oranges.

That tree reminded us of a kind, shapely, and well-dressed lady, so we called her Nanny Tree. We loved her and felt certain she loved us in return. But her watchful owner was a problem.

Late one evening, acting on a secret plan, Pat and I sneaked out of the house and made our way across the property line to Nanny Tree.

The oranges were ripe, their brilliant colour glowing in the dark. The lower part of the tree was surrounded by tall grass and shrubs, but on our earlier visits, we had created a narrow path through them, like a short tunnel leading to the open space below the tree.

"You go in through the grass," Pat whispered, reminding me of the plan. "I'll hit the branches with the stick, and when the oranges fall, you pick them up."

For a moment I felt irritated and longed for the day when I'd be big enough to be the one wielding the stick and Pat the one forced to crawl on hands and knees. But right now she was taller and stronger.

Pat proceeded to whack the bunches of fruit from their branches while I crawled into the darkness under the tree.

My senses came alive in the dark. I smelled the powerful fragrance of the oranges every time my sister's stick made contact with the branches and heard the soft thud of the oranges as they hit the ground.

I felt my way around the ground in the dark, joyfully scooping up oranges one by one and dropping them into the front of my bunched-up skirt.

I was so intent on what I was doing that I didn't hear the telltale sounds until they joined together into a loud, buzzing roar.

It came at me from all sides. A swarm of angry bees.

My feet soon found the open space in the thick grass, and I quickly backed out through it. My sister, unaware of the bees now swarming around my face, neck, and arms, kept pushing me back in, telling me to pick up more of the oranges. Howling, I finally broke free. My upper body was covered with bees.

We stumbled back home in the dark, oranges long forgotten, my sister saying, "Shut up, shut up – remember, we were stealing," whenever I cried out in pain. I do not remember sleeping that night, and it seemed my sister, too, was awake. Every time I started to whimper or cry out loud, she covered my mouth softly with her hand and urgently pleaded for me to keep quiet.

It was no use. The next day, my face, arms, and neck were covered with the evidence of my crime. My mother listened to the story without scolding us, and when she wrapped her arms around me I thought I saw tears escaping her eyes. That had a bigger impact on me than any punishment. I had never seen my mother cry.

I promised myself then that I would never steal the neighbours' fruit again. And I kept my promise. For at least a week.

It must be true that children have their own guardian angels. By all reasonable estimations, at least some of the children in our family should have been seriously injured before reaching adulthood. But the worst that ever happened was that we repeatedly got stings, cuts, and bruises – and painful infections between our toes – and had to suffer through the remedies, which seemed just as painful.

~

As we children played, or snuggled into our beds at night, strange things were taking place in the adult world.

A man had recently been sent to prison for stabbing his wife. Another man returned home after serving a long sentence for raping a woman he knew. Half a mile from our house, a third man hanged himself on the tallest, widest tree in the large field we passed every day on our way to and from school. If you didn't know about the hanging, you would have wanted to climb that tree.

The adults whispered these things to keep the children from knowing, but children have their own communication system. About twelve of us walked to and from school in a pack: my two older sisters and me, and girls and boys from four neighbouring homes.

Between all the bits we'd overheard from the adults' conversations, we settled on these facts: the man killed his wife after she did something in bed with another man; none of the adults believed that the man imprisoned for rape had really done so; and no one knew why the other man had hanged himself, but everyone now said that the tree was unlucky. A long time ago, another man had hanged himself on that very same tree.

Of the three brutal events, I understood only one: the hanging. The other two required a knowledge I did not yet have.

The adult world seemed full of men and their deeds and misdeeds. Women who came to Mama to have their dresses made often told her stories about their husbands or boyfriends. As Mama took out her tape measure and jotted down the size of their hips, waists, arms, bustlines, and shoulders, the women talked, sometimes ignoring a child standing nearby.

"Walls have ears," my mother would warn. Her dark brown eyes tried to flash a signal to her visitor.

"Little pigs have big ears," she would say next, if the woman kept talking.

Even at six years of age, I understood my mother's signals, but some of the women didn't. My belly about to burst from trying to hold the laughter in, I finally ran out of the room.

In our father's barbershop, the men also talked about the deeds of men. I sometimes stood outside, under the window, listening to their comments about the men who wanted to rule the island or just the nearby town, about the men who had sold their land to the Alcan bauxite company, about the men who had left for jobs in England. The men's conversations were puzzling. They were never as interesting as the women's.

~

Before dinner each day, Yvonne, Pat, and I had to fetch the goats. The older girls got the bright idea one day that we could tie the goats' ropes around our waists. The goats, as though acting on a secret plan of their own, took off down the hill, dragging us along, as we screamed at the top of our lungs. We never did that again.

After dinner came the ghost stories, told by our parents or visiting uncles. The headless corpse who wandered around looking for his head. The "rolling calf," a big brute of a bull with fire in his eyes. The sneaky ghost that stole the hearts of children who had wandered too far from home.

We children gasped and squirmed as the scary story got close to the end. Then, as darkness fell, Mama sent us to wash ourselves in the outside room where the bathing and washing were done.

On the way there and back, we shrieked at every shadow and every sound. Then, when our parents had settled us down, it was time for bed. Tired from our day's adventures, safe from the responsibilities that belonged to our loving parents, we fell asleep almost as soon as our heads hit the pillows.

We didn't know that something big had already been put in motion and was about to change our world. And if we had known, we couldn't have stopped it.

For my older sisters and me, perhaps even for our little sister, Jackie, and baby brother, Michael, the pink house with the tall trees and wide stream and loving mother and father was a magical place and we expected that it would go on forever.

Chapter Two

Grandmother's House

Our grandmother lived in a big house a mile up the road. She didn't have to go outside to bathe because she had an inside bathroom.

It had the first flush toilet we'd ever seen. We children lined up to use the bathroom just to be able to pull the chain that brought water flooding into the toilet bowl.

The house, Mama said, had been handed down from our grandfather's side of the family, which, just two generations before, had owned almost all of the land in the district.

Each time the house changed hands, another room was added. By the time I was six, the house had a front verandah and several spacious rooms, including a front parlour with dark old-time furniture, crocheted white doilies, and pink and yellow plastic roses in a vase on the antique centre table. Hardly anyone sat in that room. Mostly, it was used when special people – adults – came to visit.

For us children, the nicest thing about visiting our grandmother's home – next to flushing the toilet – was the certain knowledge that we wouldn't have to stay for long. We could hardly wait to return home. For one thing, our father never came with us on these visits to his mother-in-law. He always had a reason for staying home. For another, this house was full of rules.

Grandmother Artress did not have a way with children. She was a big, stern woman, who wore spectacles and had false teeth that seemed very big as she spoke to us in commandments.

"You will not do that!" she hollered as one of us flushed the toilet for the second time.

"You must not do that!" she commanded if we laughed too loudly, especially when she was talking.

Our mother's mother rarely laughed in our presence and saw no reason why children should laugh in her presence either.

One day, our very proper grandmother broke wind. We knew that people did this. We children certainly did it. But if the queen of England had come for lunch and done it, we couldn't have been more amazed that day.

Our grandmother also seemed caught by surprise and tried to stop it in mid-sound, but it was too late.

"Poong-choooo!"

The sound filled the room and seemed to continue for a very long time.

We knew it was impolite to notice. But we couldn't help it this time. We laughed till tears streamed down our faces and our stomachs hurt.

Our grandmother didn't laugh. Acting as though she hadn't just released a very rude amount of air from her bottom, she gave us a lecture to bring us into line.

"It's not everything you should laugh at," she said. "Polite children do not laugh at such things."

As we stared at her, trying our best to squelch our laughter, but failing, she told us a story.

"One day a young woman applied for a job. The man who was interviewing her passed gas, just to see how she'd react. She laughed a loud laugh. Well, what do you think happened?" she asked, peering down at us through her eyeglasses.

We couldn't imagine what happened, and she didn't stop long enough for us to answer.

"She didn't get the job. The manager knew right there and then that she didn't have good manners."

We tried and tried but still could not stop giggling.

"Children should be seen and not heard," my sisters and I would say when we got back home, mimicking the way our grandmother looked and sounded when she told us these words.

"A whistling woman and a crowing hen are an abomination to the Lord!" my eldest sister Yvonne would add, recalling the time our grandmother caught us on her verandah trying to whistle.

But nothing made an impact like poong-choooo. On a rainy day when we were stuck inside our house, any of us children could reduce the others to helpless laughter just by uttering that one word.

Though a strict disciplinarian herself, our mother was quick to laugh. People smiled in her presence.

Mama's mother, Artress, seemed her opposite in every way. A towering presence in any room she entered, she was a woman used to being obeyed by those around her, a woman whom people respected and perhaps even feared, but – I was sure – did not love.

I was just too small, too powerless in her presence, to comprehend that anyone could love my grandmother. But despite some disagreements, her sons seemed to love her. And years before, Mama said, someone else had loved her fiercely. My grandfather Victor.

"We lost Papa when I was young," our mother told us one day after we visited our grandmother's home. "He was a loving man, a really loving father."

We had heard little about our grandfather and hadn't thought to ask till now.

"He was a brilliant man who invented things," Mama continued, noting our keen interest. "He was a goldsmith. He made or repaired jewelry, watches, and clocks. He had his own business. He and Mama were a real match for each other. Both were very intelligent."

"Where did he go?" we asked.

"He died," Mama replied, her face suddenly sad. "He died when I was just a girl. Fell on a wet pavement one night, hit his head, and later died in his sleep."

We were speechless, lost in imagining how our mother must have felt to lose her father.

"Ah, my dear children," Mama sighed, after a moment of gazing into the distance. "You just never know what life has in store."

I felt a tingle on my arm, as if one of the spirits from our parents' ghost stories had reached out and touched me.

Chapter Three

Paradise Lost

One day, while our father was cutting a customer's hair in his barbershop, Mama gathered us in the dining room and gave us the news.

Our father was going away.

We were stricken with shock, then fear. The questions tumbled out of our mouths before she could say more.

"Where, Mama?"

"When, Mama?"

"Why, Mama?"

"For how long, Mama?"

Mama answered our questions slowly, trying to calm our fears. He was going to England, she said, forcing the words out of her mouth. He would be leaving within a few weeks. He was going there to work.

None of this made any sense, even to my older sisters. For one thing, our father already worked.

Mama paused, looking for a way to explain this awful thing.

"Your father and I work very hard," she said. "You know this; you see us every day."

We nodded in quick agreement. Every night when we went to bed, she was still in the dining room, sewing.

Despite all their hard work, she said, if they continued as they were, the two of them would never earn enough money to build a proper house for our family.

But this made no sense either. Our house was perfect. Why did we need another?

"Our house is too small and rickety for all of us," she said. "You girls are getting older. We need more space."

I was still thinking about this second bit of awful news when Mama said there was plenty of work in England. Our father could earn enough money in a few years to build the new house.

"Your father is going to travel on a ship to England," she said.

We stared at her, our eyes even wider now.

"The same ship that took my brothers safely to England."

This last bit was meant to reassure us, but it didn't work. Our uncles had never returned.

My older sisters and I began to cry. Our younger sister, Jackie, wasn't old enough to understand why we were crying, but realizing something was wrong, she burst into tears. Our baby brother, Michael, stopped crawling around the shiny dark wooden floor and started to wail. Mama picked him up and tried to soothe him.

There was worse to come, and we got the news days after. This time, both parents broke it to us.

We would have to leave our home soon, they said. While our father was away, we would live with our grandmother.

"It won't be for long," they kept saying. "It will help our family to save money. And then we will have our own new house."

The last words were said over the sound of children's sobs.

My mother's eyes glistened, and, for only the second time in my life, I was sure I saw her start to cry.

One day, a woman who came to pick up her dress chatted with Mama about the changes affecting families like ours.

"It's not just our district, you know," I heard her say. Some of the men leaving for England were young and unmarried, but many, like our father, were leaving a wife and children behind. It was the only way to get ahead.

In our father's barbershop, a similar conversation was taking place about the changes going on across the island, changes that sometimes seemed to contradict each other. Learned Jamaican men made loud speeches about the need for Jamaica to be independent from Britain, while tens of thousands of Jamaican men quietly packed their bags and left for jobs there.

"It's all for the better," my usually stern grandmother had said, bidding goodbye to yet another son, not knowing whether she would ever see him again.

"It's all for the better," my mother's customers said, consoling her about the upcoming departure of her husband.

"It's all for the better," adult relatives told us, patting our heads. "You're too young to understand right now, but you'll see."

"The fatherland," one of the adults called England, and now I knew why. England was the place where the fathers went.

Our father started packing a plaid, hard-shell suitcase, the kind everyone called a grip. Our mother helped him pack his clothes, shoes, toiletries, Bible, photos of the family. One night, a few weeks later, he hugged and kissed us all before bedtime. The next morning, while we were still asleep, he picked up his grip, walked out the door, and headed for the bus to Kingston where his ship was waiting.

Chapter Four

A House Full of Women

Everything I did was wrong.

I don't recall the day of the uprooting, the day we left the little pink house and stream and trees behind, but I remember this: everything I did, once we entered our grandmother's house, was wrong.

We children tried especially hard to mind our manners. But every time one of us spoke too loud, laughed too loud, or ran through the house, an angry look came over my grandmother's face.

For having raised "little pigs," for having turned out children "with absolutely no manners," our mother got the brunt of our grandmother's fury. At first, Grandmother chastised her in loud whispers. But within a few days, this courtesy had fallen by the wayside: she corrected us and then admonished Mama right in front of us.

One day, when I'd almost gotten used to this treatment, she said an astonishing thing.

"If you'd had the good sense to marry a better man," she told my mother, "I wouldn't have to put up with you and your unruly children."

Things that had never made sense before suddenly did. Now I knew why our father had never visited our grandmother when the rest of the family did: our grandmother didn't like him, didn't think he was good enough for a son-in-law.

Mama didn't fight back. For a moment she looked as though about to cry. But she just turned away.

Waves of intense emotions washed over me: shame for my mother, who seemed to have been stripped of all her clothing; a fierce desire to protect her; and a pure, unfiltered hatred for my grandmother. I wanted to kick my grandmother's shins, scratch her face, and yell the rudest words I could find. But even then, at seven years old, I knew this would only cause my mother more pain. Now it was my turn to stay silent.

It seemed that, in our grandmother's eyes, we children were useful for only two things: fetching items she needed from another part of a room, and performing the dreaded pinning.

Our grandmother had a shower in her bathroom but refused to use it. Instead, she soaked herself in a huge tin bathtub placed on the floor of her large bedroom at the back of the house.

"Children," she'd call, since she couldn't remember our names. "One of you! Come here this minute!"

We all went running the first time, all except Michael, the baby. Lounging in her bath was our naked grandmother. We had never seen an adult naked, and definitely not one with such huge breasts. Frightened by the sight, we ran back out, trembling, and refused to re-enter the room. Mama finally made Yvonne, our eldest sister, go back in and hand Grandmother the towel she had forgotten to place within reach of the bath.

Minutes later, Yvonne had to go back in again.

"Pin me up!" our grandmother ordered.

Grandmother needed someone to pin her brassiere at the back. She had sewn the brassiere herself from very strong white cotton, but the hooks, protesting against the size and weight of her massive breasts, sometimes gave way. Unwilling to trust them, she had resorted to using two large safety pins to hold the ends of the bra together, but since the ends met in the middle of her back, she needed someone else to fasten it. Every day.

There was no use protesting. The task fell to Yvonne, then, months later, to Pat, then finally to me. By the time I was eight, I was pinning the brassiere daily.

But before the pinning came another ritual. My grandmother wielded a round pink powder puff to pat the space between and under her breasts with something that smelled like baby powder. Then she dabbed Khus Khus perfume on her neck and behind her ears. But no fragrance could make bearable the long minutes of standing alone in a bedroom with a woman I hated, a woman whose breasts and brassiere proved that she belonged to a different species from mine.

~

My grandmother's house was a world of women, a world without adult men.

My eldest uncle had stayed in Jamaica. He and his family lived in a hillside house up the road. On his way to or from work, flying by on his powerful shiny black motorcycle, he waved to us and blew his horn but rarely stopped. I wished he would because he was bright and funny and always made our mother laugh.

On the occasions when he did stop, my sisters and I begged him to take us for a ride, and once in a while, he and Mama agreed. An older child hopped onto the motorcycle and hugged our uncle's back, while he lifted a younger child to snuggle into his chest. Then the bike flew down the road as though with wings. Nothing – not even climbing tall trees and swinging like Tarzan – equalled the terror and joy of those rides.

But our uncle and his mother seemed incapable of being together for more than a few minutes without a terrible argument erupting.

Always, the fight was over God. A deaconess in the church that she had helped to establish, my grandmother strongly believed in the goodness of God. My uncle didn't, and there was nothing she could do about it.

Even back then, I knew that he loved her and all of us. And we loved him back. But the hostilities between him and his mother finally got to him. One day, he walked into the village square with a Bible, and, certain that all eyes were on him, tore it to shreds.

A shocked hush fell over everyone watching, even my grandmother. After that, it was a very long time before my uncle even stopped in front of the house. The motorbike seemed to gather even more speed as it flew through the village.

In the oppressive atmosphere of our grandmother's house, as our beloved mother grew sadder and quieter, I dreamed. Criticized daily by my grandmother, deprived of the company of the only uncle living nearby, and surrounded by more houses, more people, more religion, and more rules, I dreamed. That one day we'd be the same family that lived in the same little pink house with the stream and trees. I imagined them missing us, waiting for our return, as we missed our father and uncles and waited for their return.

Chapter Five

Angels Passing Through

In spite of everything, those years in our grandmother's home were years of learning and discovery, of growing into the selves we were going to be.

My sisters and I coped the best we could. We tried to be obedient to our mother. We tried to behave ourselves so we wouldn't upset our grandmother. Then we went and climbed the tallest trees we could find on our grandmother's property and her next-door neighbours'.

"Bet you can't climb that tall plantain tree right next to the fence line," Pat taunted me one day, just months after we moved in.

And so we continued our brave feats, some of which defied sanity. I climbed the plantain tree as Pat and our cousin Bev watched from below. Its smooth trunk and lack of branches had defeated all challengers, even Pat. Slowly, very carefully, I kept going till I made it to the top. It was a special moment. I felt extraordinarily proud, and in that moment of supreme confidence and joy, I let go of the tree ever so slightly.

And then I slipped and plunged into the barbed wire fence below, ripping open the side of my leg till I could see the white cartilage through the blood. Pat and Bev helped me home, one on each side. All I could think of in that moment was something my grandmother had told me just that morning: "Pride goeth before a fall."

Mama told us later that she felt faint when she saw the length of the gash, but that there was so much blood pouring down my leg, she had no time to pass out.

Our grandmother seemed the least shocked by what had happened. Although I was the only grandchild who dared talk back to her, the one who still disliked her, I knew this much: she knew things. There were times when she'd stop suddenly, as though listening to an invisible companion. Then, using plain words or a proverb, she'd warn me against doing some mischief that I was secretly planning. The morning before the terrible fall from the plantain tree had been one of those times.

You'd think that would have stopped me from climbing trees. It didn't. Once my leg healed, Pat and I were back at it.

"Bet you can't ..." were still fighting words. Once they'd been uttered, Pat and I climbed anything and everything. Once I even climbed the light pole on the roadside in front of our house, as my younger sister Jackie and brother Michael watched from below.

My mother caught me in the act. I was shocked to learn that the electric wires were "live" and that I had narrowly escaped electrocution. As I climbed down, I saw the fright in my siblings' eyes and felt ashamed of myself. I was their older sister and I had frightened them.

That Good Friday, we were taken to church to sit through a long, horrible service in which Jesus was marched to the place of his crucifixion, his side and forehead bleeding. The minister told us that "Jesus gave his life for ours" and we were to repent of our sins. I wholeheartedly repented of two: my pride and frightening Jackie and Michael.

When we went to church on Easter Sunday and Jesus mysteriously rose from the grave, I felt certain that my repentance had helped him do it.

We returned home that Easter to another mystery. Tiny flowers, like the kind fairies would have in their garden, were blooming under a window by the front of the house. They were pink, mauve, yellow, and white. Not knowing what they were and why they were there, we children immediately called them Easter lilies, figuring they were somehow connected to the resurrection of Jesus. They bloomed every Easter during the years we lived with our grandmother, their mystery never lessening.

Our grandmother's house was a mysterious place.

Sometimes, a gentle breeze ruffled the still air inside the house and something invisible seemed to float in, something none of us children could explain, something that came from another world.

"Hekkentiyah sattray!" our grandmother would exclaim, her entire body focused on something we couldn't see.

We had no idea what these words meant, but after it happened a few times, we knew the words that would follow right after: "Angel passing through!"

And then, she would take one of us by the shoulder, and quickly, gently, spin us around a few times. And then we'd sit and wait politely for the angel to leave the room.

I don't recall exactly when I realized that there were two kinds of beings in our home: humans that you could see with your own eyes and beings that only certain people could see. Our mother and grandmother saw the invisible people and even spoke to them at times.

First, there were "the Father, the Son, and the Holy Ghost," to whom they spoke regularly, not just when we went to church. They called out to one or all of them in times of trouble, and they thanked them whenever someone they loved recovered from a serious illness, or even for something simple, like a meal or a safe journey.

"Thank you, God, for journeying mercies," my mother or grandmother would say whenever a family member returned home safely from a trip that required travel in a car or bus.

But some spirits were not welcome in our home.

When any of us visited a home where someone had recently died, there was one thing we had to do before re-entering our house: turn around three times.

"Why do we always have to do this?" I asked Mama one evening after she'd stopped me from turning the knob of our front door and going inside. We'd gone to visit a neighbour who had lost her sister.

"So any ghost who's following us will get confused and wander away," she said, as we turned around on the dark verandah.

"Why do ghosts get confused when we turn?" I started to ask as I completed my last turn. But my mother was already opening the door. I didn't want to be left outside in the dark with a confused ghost, not for even a second, so I hurried inside, almost tripping over my own feet.

One of us must have forgotten to do this simple thing after our relative Nellie died. She used to visit our home whenever she had troubles, and my mother always gave her a meal and words of advice.

When she suddenly died, Nellie's ghost returned to the place where she had always received comfort: our home. Mama shared the news of her return, then continued with her sewing, hemming a dress and talking to Nellie as though she were sitting right beside her.

Mama encouraged her to leave, but Nellie didn't like this advice. Instead, she chose a bed to sleep in at night: the children's bed where all the girls slept. One night, Nellie pushed each child out of bed, and then, early in the morning, when I climbed back in, she lay on top of me till I screamed.

Mama was sympathetic to some ghosts, but this one had gone too far. It had attacked her children.

"Nellie, I know you're afraid to leave," my mother said firmly, looking straight at the invisible spirit. Then, raising her voice, she continued, "but now it's time to get out of this house and go 'bout your own business. You can't be troubling my children, pushing them out of their own bed!"

Mama's voice deepened to an almost-growl.

"You're dead, Nellie! It's time to move on. You don't belong here. Get out of this house. Right now!"

Nellie never bothered us again, and Mama never had to order a ghost out of our house again. At least not while we children watched.

Other mysteries were taking place. Yvonne was quietly changing as she went through a thing our grandmother called puberty, becoming more sedate. None of us children knew how to talk about these changes, so we didn't.

Our mother didn't know how to handle the topic of puberty either. One day she came home with a big book titled *On Becoming a Woman*. Pat and I looked at the pictures, rolling our eyes and making gagging noises, but Yvonne became absorbed in the book. It was yet another sign that she was becoming less a daredevil and more a young lady.

At age nine, I took the scholarship exam for high school and soon after entered a land of giants. Pat was in a higher grade, ready to defend me from the teasing laughter of older children. They didn't understand why such a small child was in high school or why I was so "lippy."

Nor, it appeared, did the teachers, who regularly sent me to the headmaster's office for "insubordination," which meant I'd argued with them or not listened, due to daydreaming. For a while, I seemed to spend more time in the headmaster's office than in class.

Stranger things happened as the years sped by, some better and some worse. My first menstrual period came, followed by signs that the two little bumps on my chest were getting bigger.

Did these things run in families, I wondered? Remembering our grandmother's huge breasts, I prayed that God would spare me a similar affliction.

And then, deciding that it wasn't too late for Yvonne and Pat, I closed my eyes again and prayed for them, too.

Chapter Six

Stick a Pin There

For weeks, my mother sewed a wedding dress for a beautiful young woman who worked in an office in the nearby town.

"Can we see the dress, Mama? Can we please see the dress?" we asked every day when we came home from school.

Day by day, my sisters and I watched the long white bridal dress become the prettiest thing we had ever seen. Even our young brother, not normally interested in women's things, took notice as Mama carefully added the lace and beads. She had never made such a fancy dress before, and it seemed to me she was putting more love into this dress than any other.

Mama had known the bride since she was a child, had watched her grow up, applauded her hard work and excellent results at school, and rejoiced when she got a job with a prestigious firm. Now the young woman was getting married, and Mama was happy.

We were mesmerized not only by the dress, but also by the bride herself. Everything about her seemed perfect: smooth brown skin, a perfect figure, big bright eyes, a beautifully shaped nose and mouth, lustrous, immaculately groomed black hair. Happiness made her seem even more beautiful.

I used to linger near the sewing room when she came for a fitting and listen to her chat with my mother. Gradually, I saw that these conversations were much more than happy chatter. My mother was grooming the young woman for marriage into an upper-class family. She came from a poor family and wanted to make a good impression on her future in-laws. Mama gave her tips about marriage, etiquette, and how to run a household.

The bridegroom-to-be was a young lawyer, and from everything we overheard, he adored his intended. My older sisters and I could only dream that one day we would meet someone who would love us as much. Meantime, we lived vicariously through this young bride-to-be, admiring her every move.

The day of the final fitting arrived. The bride was late. An hour passed, then two. She finally arrived, in tears. My mother, usually quick to usher us children out when a friend or customer arrived with a problem, rushed to the young woman's side, forgetting that I was in the room.

"Oh, m'dear, m'dear," she said. "Nothing could be that bad."

Mama handed her a small cloth handkerchief and made her sit on the sofa and sip lemonade.

Bit by bit, the story came out: The young woman and her fiancé had not revealed her background to his family until just weeks before the wedding. They, shocked that such a beautiful and well-dressed young woman was not from "a good family," responded by rejecting her outright and forcing their son to call the wedding off.

The parents were staunch members of a prominent church and claimed they supported equality for all. To avoid charges of hypocrisy, they let it be known that they had heard something disgraceful about the young woman, without ever explaining what.

A young woman's dreams were shattered.

My mother held her hands, hugged her, prayed with her. It seemed to take hours for the sobbing to subside.

Meanwhile, our family took the news as though it had happened to us. My mother was especially angry. She had often said to us, "This girl is proof that with hard work and opportunity, any person can work their way out of the humblest circumstances."

When her visitor finally left, eyes red from weeping, my mother went to her bedroom and closed the door. She stayed there for a long time. Finally I knocked. Hearing no response, I gently opened the door. Mama was on her knees, praying. She sounded like she was arguing with God. She was also crying.

It was only the third time that I saw my mother cry. Even when our grandmother humiliated her, even the day our father left for England, she had held back her tears, putting on a brave face in front of the children.

I closed the door quickly before she could see me.

"Stick a pin there," my mother used to tell me when I had a thought worth remembering.

I stuck a pin on this day. It was the day I learned that people were divided in different ways, and some of the divisions could hurt, badly. The size of a family's house mattered. Who your parents were, whether they owned land, and what they did for a living mattered. The shade of your skin mattered. I just couldn't figure out how these things determined whether you were seen as coming from a good home or a bad one.

Chapter Seven

A Home of Our Own

Time rolled on, and my older sisters became young women. Our father had now been in England for several years.

Pat, the former tomboy, had become an outstanding beauty and had gone off to secretarial school. Yvonne had grown into a pretty, ladylike young woman, and was engaged to a handsome young man from a few villages away. The wedding was a joyful event.

As our big sister drove off to begin her new life, Pat and I joked that she had gotten married early so she would never ever have to pin our grandmother's brassiere again. That brassiere had become the butt of many jokes through the years.

I suffered through being the smallest child in every one of my high school classes, but learned to stand up for myself by developing a sharp tongue. Those frequent moments of disgrace – the times I'd been sent to the headmaster's office – had unintended consequences. The headmaster loved a good debate and found something for us to argue about on every visit. Soon he encouraged me to join the school's debating team.

For weeks after I joined the team, I was a disembodied

voice, the only debater whose face couldn't be seen above the podium. Finally, somebody brought me a wooden box to stand on. The audience laughed and cheered before I'd said a single word.

Meanwhile, stuck in her mother's home, her husband still abroad, our mother found new ways to cope.

I watched her become tougher, more self-reliant. She also developed a strong faith in God. Mama bought land to build the new house, worked with the architect to develop the blueprints, hired the workers, ordered the materials, and supervised the builders while cooking a robust lunch for them every day.

She did all this while running a household, raising children, and managing her sewing business. It all seemed to put a steel rod in her spine. Now she regularly stood up to her mother, defending her husband's good name or supporting her children against unwarranted criticism.

That, in turn, caused her mother to change. She criticized less and seemed to listen more.

Meanwhile, our father was working two jobs in London: he was a porter on the railway by day and a barber by night. Since we had no telephone, my mother never heard his voice during those years. They communicated only through their letters.

Every two weeks, like clockwork, Mama or one of the older children went to the post office a mile away, where the postmistress handed over the light-blue envelope from our father, bearing a letter and money order. We never saw him during those years. Had he come home to visit, the expense would have delayed the completion of the house and his permanent return. In her letters to him, Mama told him all about the house. She wanted it to seem real to him so far away in cold, wet England.

We counted down the time that he would be returning based on what remained to be built. The roof, plumbing, and wiring were finished. Now our father had to pay for the windows and doors, and the bathroom fixtures. After that it was the kitchen cupboards, and the tiling for the floors.

Finally, after nine years of sacrifice, the house was completed. Unlike the tiny pink house, made of wood, this two-storey structure was made of concrete, and its exterior walls were a sandy beige. Set on a hillside, it had a spacious verandah, a living room and dining room, three bedrooms, and a family bathroom, with more rooms roughed in downstairs in case our family needed them one day.

The kitchen and dining room had louvered glass windows that looked down over the trees on our land and all the way down the green valley below. The rooms smelled of fresh paint. The whole house was bright. As far as I could tell, there were no ghosts there.

Mama had farmed when we lived at the pink house, and now she once again had enough land to plant fruit trees, grow yams and sweet potatoes, and keep chickens, goats, and pigs.

The big day came, almost exactly ten years after our father had left us. He returned home at last to shouts and tears of joy, carrying the same plaid hard-shell grip that he'd taken with him to England. Now it contained gifts for Mama and each child. A second suitcase held his suits and other items.

It was surprising how little he had changed. He was still a handsome man, his clothes indicated an excellent sense of style, and his manners were impeccable. He was still quick to smile and chat with neighbours.

He told us about London. The house where he lived among strangers. The cold weather. The colour and class prejudice. His first sight of Buckingham Palace. The railway station where he worked.

Prince Philip had come to that station one day, and our father carried his bags. The prince, said my father, had "treated him like a human being."

This, it seemed, was our father's proudest moment in England.

Mama was impressed, moved. But I felt embarrassed for my father. I couldn't meet his eyes.

Three months passed.

Our father had taken small black-and-white photos of his family with him to England, of Mama, his beautiful, shapely, vivacious wife, still in her early thirties; of a baby boy and four older children, all under the age of thirteen; of him and Mama together.

I came across him one day when he was quietly looking at the photos. Their scalloped edges were worn as though he had touched them every day over ten years.

But the people in those photos were now ghosts of a different time. For him and for us, so much had taken place, we hardly knew where to begin, which stories to tell, which pain to hide or reveal. He'd come back to a country that was now proudly independent of Britain. But worst of all, he'd come back to a family who'd grown independent of him.

Our father discovered that our home was now a place of strong women and one adolescent boy. None of us remembered what it was like to have an adult man in the home.

Though everyone tried hard to adjust to the new situation, it was a rough transition.

Mama went out of her way to cede leadership of the family to him at certain times, completely forgetting his presence at other times and having to backtrack, apologetic. Our father seemed overwhelmed by her strength.

The tension became so thick, it felt like a physical presence in the house. Everyone tried to make a wide berth around it, afraid that if we accidentally bumped into it, something would break.

I was sixteen, already graduated from high school and feeling grown up. My manner was that of an adult, but the words that flew out of my mouth in the middle of one stormy argument were anything but.

"We were doing just fine before you came home!"

I hurled the words at my father. He almost sagged against the doorway where he stood.

It was an awful thing to say to a man who had sacrificed so much for his family. Shocked, he replied just as angrily.

I was still livid, but I knew I had crossed a terrible line.

In her bedroom, just minutes later, my mother packed her best travel bag with a few precious items, keepsakes meant to remind me that, despite the awful quarrel, I was loved. She also gave me all the cash she had in her purse: two dollars. We both tried to hold back the tears as I hugged her goodbye.

I was leaving home, but my mother and I both knew I'd be safe. Surprising even myself, I was going to the one place I'd spent years wanting to escape.

Chapter Eight

I See My Grandmother Differently

When I was seven years old, I saw everything in black and white. My mother was good. My grandmother was bad. End of story.

By the time I was twelve, I began to see things I had never even thought of before. Like what a big strain the arrival of our family had placed on my grandmother. As the "few years" of our father's absence stretched into five, then nearly ten, I even empathized with her. But I still didn't love her.

Gradually, and very reluctantly, I grew to respect her instead. I realized that, in spite of her imperious manner, there was a whole other side to her that I hadn't taken the time to see.

Mama had always taught us, especially when we children quarrelled, to try to see the other person's point of view. But I didn't know what it was like to be an adult, especially one like my grandmother.

I had thought her harsh and even cruel, but as the years passed, I began to notice things. Grandmother was a nurse at the local infirmary. When she worked the evening shift, my older sisters and I brought her the hot meal that Mama made for her. Those visits to the local infirmary revealed an entirely different part of her personality. She treated the patients in her care with affection and respect. And there were countless stories in our village of how our grandmother had helped others through bad times.

Then my classmate Jenny died after having a fever. Seeing my grief and shock, my grandmother insisted that we go together to say goodbye to her at the family home where her body lay. The very thought terrified me. I had never seen a dead person before.

During the visit, my grandmother held my hand, said a fervent prayer for my friend, and helped me whisper words of goodbye. Walking home on the dark, unpaved road, she again drew me close, talking the whole time to drive away my fears. That night she said a strange thing to me.

"You are going to be a special person," she said, squeezing my hand. "You are going to be somebody."

Surprised, I said nothing. But when we came to the front door of our house and performed the usual ritual – turning around three times to prevent the ghost from accompanying us inside – something felt different. A small truce had been declared between my grandmother and me, an invisible link forged on our walk down that dark road.

Now, I was sixteen and had graduated from high school. While I hoped to go abroad to study, I had no idea how that was going to be accomplished. Worse, I had just been disgracefully rude to my father.

When my mother asked, "Where are you going?" I had immediately mentioned the only person who I knew for sure would take me in: my grandmother.

Grandmother listened to my explanation and took me into her home. Which isn't to say it was an easy time. She was still a force to be reckoned with, a woman who knew her mind.

My grandmother had not approved of her daughter's choice of husband. One day, in frustration and anger, she had insulted both my mother and father with one single hurtful sentence. Perhaps back then she had wished she could take the words back. And perhaps she was remembering this awful moment when I landed on her doorstep and confessed to the hurtful words I'd thrown at my father.

I thought I sensed a flash of empathy in her eyes, but if there was sympathy there, I didn't feel it. Before she even let me into her house, she lowered the boom on me.

"You were wrong," she told me plainly. "There is no excusing what you said."

I looked down at the verandah floor.

"You put yourself in that man's place," she continued, forcing me to look her in the eye. "You put yourself in his place and tell me how you'd feel."

I got the message, loud and clear.

~

We argued about everything, including the Bible. I now openly questioned its authority, a fact that would have horrified her a decade earlier. Now she argued back but also listened respectfully.

We sat on her verandah and argued passionately late into the evening. She loved debating, and she loved engaging with young people. Sometimes, exhausted from debating a point, neither one us prepared to give in, we looked at each other and laughed.

When my best friends from the local youth club – all teenage boys – walked me home after evening meetings, I often went to bed, leaving them on the verandah with my grandmother. As I drifted off to sleep, I heard my friends' voices as they debated politics, religion, gender roles – anything and everything – with her.

This continued for months. Then the tongue wagging began. A rumour was making the rounds in the village that young men were following me home and staying there till late at night.

The evening my grandmother heard about it, she called on all the neighbours she could find and invited them to meet her in the village square. Men, women, and even some children gathered just before dusk. My grandmother was a powerful and influential person in this village, and they wanted to find out why she had summoned them.

Wearing a belted long brown dress, her spectacles in place, her greying hair combed back into a bun, she pulled herself to her full height and spoke in a commanding voice. I was standing beside her.

"I understand that some of you are calling my grand-daughter's name into question," she said.

Silence from the crowd.

"I'll have you know – I will not put up with this for one minute longer!"

I suspected that my grandmother already knew who the main culprits were, but nipping the rumour in the bud meant the whole village needed to hear her speech.

"Yes, there are young men coming to my house at night once a week. They are members of my granddaughter's youth club. Intelligent young people, every one of them. They sit on my verandah, talking about all kinds of things, and I am grateful for the things they tell me. We old people need to know what the younger ones are thinking."

Some people shuffled their feet, crossed their arms, and looked away from her eyes. But she wasn't done.

"Some of you people have twisted this innocent thing and used it to tarnish my granddaughter's name," she growled.

No one moved. No one breathed.

"Well, let me tell you something," said my grandmother, the respected nurse and long-time church deaconess. "If those young men are having improper relations with anyone in my house, it's me!"

After a few nervous laughs, the crowd cheered her loudly.

"Amen, Sister Reid!" said an elderly man.

"Tell them, Deaconess!" said a young woman.

A few people slinked away into the gathering dusk.

My grandmother had taken on the whole village to defend my honour, and in that moment I knew it: she loved me, and I loved her.

~

Within days, I started going home to visit my parents. For one thing, I missed them. For another, I needed to apologize. Haltingly, awkwardly, I did so.

The third reason was more practical: I was hungry. My grandmother and I were both terrible cooks. The cooking gene seemed to have passed us by. After eating some of the meals we cooked, there was nothing we could do but laugh.

The one time we tried to bake a cake, the cake caught fire, leaving a black, charred mess for us to clean up. Later that day, my grandmother and I arrived at a simple truth: there are some things in this life that certain people in this world should never even attempt.

More and more, I showed up at my parents' home just in time for supper. "What brings you here, my daughter?" my mother always teased.

"I just happened to be in the neighbourhood," I always replied, smiling back at her.

Every time, after we ate, my mother packed a care package of dinner and other things for my grandmother. At last their own relationship was also getting better.

One day, as our father took his place at the head of the dinner table, as our mother said the grace, I looked at my parents, really looked at them. My eyes filled with tears of gratitude. I never moved back in with my parents, but I understood them better.

When you're little, you see some things but miss a lot of others. Now it was as clear as daylight. My parents and grandparents weren't rich or famous. They were just extraordinary.

Chapter Nine

Seed Money

Ken was my mother's younger first cousin. Tall, handsome, and stylish, much older than I, Ken was an intelligent, well-read man who challenged me with provocative arguments. Even when I was in my early teens, he treated me like an adult. When I announced proudly that I'd become an atheist, he, certainly no God-fearing man himself, forced me to defend my decision.

What made me so sure there was no God? Was it possible that I, in the throes of teenage rebellious anger at my family's church, was throwing God out with the baptismal water?

We debated the divinity of Jesus, the authenticity of the Bible, and the messy politics that ruled Jamaica. Back and forth we went. Back and forth. Argument. Counter-argument. A new perspective introduced. Common ground sometimes reached.

Together, we dreamed of things way beyond the world of our small-town upbringing. We dared question current wisdom, the unquestionable. We shared magnificent dreams of travelling to foreign lands.

As I grew older, I realized that Ken and I, apart from being each other's favourite, had something else in common. Even in the racial confusion of our African-European-Chinese-Middle Eastern extended family, Ken and I were oddities. He belonged to the mostly Chinese branch of the family, but unlike his black-haired parents and most of his siblings, his hair was light brown. With flaming reddish hair, I, too, stood out from my immediate relatives. We were genetic throwbacks to fair-haired European ancestors, but had the facial or body types of the other races that made up our family.

Ken and I were both fascinated by our extended family, and vowed that, one day, we'd write a book about it.

We had an unspoken deal. I would do well in school, and contain my impatience with the adults around me, and he would give me a special birthday gift every year. My first camera. My first pair of slingback dress shoes with matching handbag, both in yellow patent leather – the epitome of style back then.

On my fifteenth birthday, just weeks before my graduation from high school, Ken had shown up mysteriously empty-handed.

"We're going into town," he said. "Get in the car."

We parked in front of the squat, white building in Mandeville that housed the local branch of the Royal Bank of Canada.

"In a few weeks, you'll be graduating from high school," he said. "Every young lady should have a bank account."

And so, this scrawny, rebellious teenager was marched inside the bank manager's office, where Ken started a savings account in my name and made the initial deposit: one thousand dollars.

It was a fortune. The Jamaican dollar in the late sixties was worth about $1.25 US.

I was choked up with gratitude.

"Use your money wisely," was all Ken said.

In return, I made a solemn promise to him that I would "do something really, really meaningful" with my life. And one day I would also help him write "that book about our crazy family."

When I got back home, everything in my life had changed. I was no longer a teenage girl trapped for life in a small town in the middle of nowhere. Suddenly, my dream of going abroad to study didn't seem quite so unreal.

Chapter Ten

Afternoon Tea

I had left high school at the end of the sixties with a well-earned reputation as a fierce debater, avid chess and table tennis player, and a voracious reader with a talent for picking arguments with people more powerful than I.

"The world can be very unkind to people who go their own way," my mother cautioned me one afternoon as we sat companionably in the living room. She had been observing me for a long moment, while I pretended that I didn't notice.

"You'll need all the education you can get. You'll need to be strong to get ahead in this world."

My great-grandfather had been a headmaster, and my mother's parents had been educated, intelligent people. My mother hadn't gone to college, but she was a brilliant woman who had studied for as long as the family's finances allowed.

I expected to attend university, but scholarships were few, and my parents had just spent every penny they owned to build a house for the family. My cousin Ken's gift was still in my bank account, but it wasn't enough. I needed to work while I figured out my future.

I applied for a job at the local telephone company in Mandeville, the largest city in our parish, and soon found myself face to face with a beautiful woman roughly the same age as my mother.

I was nervous and she saw it.

"Hello, my dear," she said warmly. "Are you here for an interview?"

I nodded and added a belated, "Yes, I am."

"My name is Claire," she said. "Claire White. Welcome."

She imbued the word with warmth, making it sound like "well-come."

"And what is your name?" she asked.

Claire White had addressed me graciously, respectfully, as if we were equals. I was so taken aback that instead of returning her gracious behaviour, I blurted out: "Claire White. Clear white. Is that your *real* name?"

She surprised me by laughing as though we were old friends. But friends we were not. Mrs. White and I came from different planets. She belonged to Mandeville's aristocracy. I, most definitely, did not.

Minutes after meeting Mrs. White, I was interviewed by the supervisor of telephone operators, and minutes after that, I was hired as a telephone operator.

When I started work, the following Monday, I was taken into an enormous room where about a dozen women sat facing a long brown and black wooden switchboard that danced with tiny lights of different colours. In front of each woman was a panel of keys, cables, and switches. The women's fingers moved nimbly, picking up slender cables and plugging them into tiny holes below each light, flicking switches forward to address the callers.

"Operatorrrr ...?" I heard the women say, over and over. "Operator. May I help you?" They sat up straight, posture dignified, and answered every call in the politest of tones. They sounded as though they had all graduated from the same finishing school.

Near the end of the switchboard sat Claire White, the woman who had greeted me with such grace. Her beauty came from her smooth skin, sleek, lustrous black hair and above-average height, but most of all, I would discover, from her kind heart and ready wit. All the women seemed to love her. They called her "Miss Claire" as a sign of affection and respect.

What I couldn't figure out was why she was working as a telephone operator. The women of Mandeville's aristocratic families did not work, as telephone operators or anything else.

This town, which is where I had attended high school, was famous for its British-ness. It was so renowned for its afternoon teas that people in other parts of the island sometimes mentioned the two in the same breath: "Oh, Mandeville: afternoon tea."

When Mandeville's upper-class ladies had tea, it was an occasion. Tea was served from heirloom floral or silver teapots nestled in antique silver trays, poured into dainty cups with handles so small that the ladies who held them had to stick a few of their fingers outward. Almost always, there were cucumber sandwiches from which a servant had carefully removed the crust to make the sandwiches seem more … more …

Truth is, I had never figured out why anyone would remove the crust from bread. My own family would have seen this as a disgraceful waste of food. This practice, in a country where many people were poor and could barely afford to buy a loaf of bread, gave me yet another reason to dislike the upper-class people of Mandeville.

I had also never forgotten the story of the jilted bride. Years later, it pained me to even think about it. As it turned out, hers was only one example of the way some citizens of Mandeville disdained those who tried to rise above their station in life, sometimes referring to them as "hurry-come-up people."

"Miss Cynthia," Claire White said to me one day during our break. "Would you like to come for afternoon tea?"

Surprised, I stared at her. But in her eyes I saw the same warm welcome with which she had greeted me on the day of my interview. I accepted.

~

Miss Claire lived in one of the better parts of town. Most of the homes in her neighbourhood had large gardens on big lots and were set far back from the road. To get to Miss Claire's house, you followed a long, narrow, tree-lined driveway up a gentle slope, and suddenly, there it was: a spacious and airy one-storey structure overlooking a large, well-tended, English-style garden lush with perennial flowers, shrubs, and fruit trees.

The house was furnished tastefully with antique furniture, English and Jamaican art, and a few Chinese and Japanese figurines.

Like my mother, Miss Claire was fond of growing things. On some of my visits, we strolled through her gardens. She was particularly fond of certain flowers, low-growing forget-me-nots and the tall-stemmed agapanthus among them.

Birds and butterflies darted to and fro among the flowerbeds. Occasionally, she stopped to talk to them.

"Good morning, little Mr. Bird," she would say to a hummingbird in the moment that it hovered in front of a red hibiscus before taking off again. "Aren't you beautiful!"

"You're looking a bit droopy today," she would note to a lily. "You need to lift up your head a bit."

To an orange tree that had borne a bountiful crop of fruit, she would say, "You've done so well, my dear tree. Thank you."

It was on one of those garden walks that she answered the question I hadn't yet found the nerve to ask.

Her husband had been a well-to-do farmer and businessman, she told me. But he had died young, leaving her with three small children. To augment her income, she worked at the telephone company. She enjoyed the women and had become skilled at handling the high-and-mighty callers who sometimes talked down to them. She had stopped one woman in the middle of a tirade simply by identifying herself in her calm and gracious manner. I smiled, picturing the caller eating humble pie.

Miss Claire's manners were always gracious, her use of the English language sophisticated, her public demeanour that of an English-Jamaican lady. One day, while I was at her home, she had an important visitor, a well-known writer. He was a tall, elegant white man, his name well known on the island for his unabashed love of patois, the Jamaican dialect. Patois was not often used in "polite company."

"Miss Cynthia, would you please do the honours?" Miss Claire asked.

Miss Claire employed a housekeeper, but she always carried out the ritual of making and serving tea herself. She had shown me how to brew tea once, and I had watched her do it countless times, but hadn't paid much attention at the time.

Now I felt grown up, pleased to be asked to do the honours.

"How do you like your tea, Mr. Maxwell?" I asked our guest.

He smiled at me charmingly.

"Strong. Thank you, m'dear," he replied.

So said, so done. I went into the kitchen, and put the kettle on.

He said "strong," I reminded myself as the kettle boiled. So I opened a large can of loose-leaf tea and emptied much of it into the teapot. Then I poured in the boiling water, covered the teapot, waited for the tea to steep, and neatly placed it and the teacups, saucers, and other tea-serving accoutrements on the silver tray.

I carried the tray slowly and carefully into the living room and placed it on a small table next to Miss Claire.

Miss Claire seemed to have been born knowing how to serve tea. Hers was a seamless mixture of skill and artistry. Lifting the teapot with one hand and pouring the tea into a cup nestled in matching saucer before handing it to her visitor – she did it in one smooth action. Not for the first time, I found myself mesmerized by the fluidity and grace of her movements.

Our guest settled back in his comfortable chair and took his first sip of the tea.

"Oh, mi gawd!" he hollered, spouting tea through his nostrils, speaking in patois. "This yeah tea could kill a hoss!"

Surprised and mystified, Miss Claire and I quickly took a sip of our tea – and realized that Mr. Maxwell was almost entirely right. The tea, at the very least, could have stopped a horse in its tracks. I'd poured in way too many tealeaves.

"I am so sorry," I apologized, ashamed of my ineptitude in Miss Claire's almost sacred ritual, the art of brewing tea.

But Miss Claire made a gentle joke, invited the famous author to talk to me about my desire to become a writer, then disappeared into the kitchen to correct my error.

A few minutes later, Mr. Maxwell sat back with his tea for the second time, enjoying it without incident.

~

There was no doubt: Claire White was the kind of woman I had come across only in books.

Unlike most women I knew, she smoked, occasionally drank wine and brandy, held modern opinions, and often wore either long dresses or loose-fitting trousers.

Born and raised in an overwhelmingly Christian country, she sometimes spoke about other religions, but only, it seemed, to people she liked and trusted.

Descended from African slaves and English slave owners, Miss Claire was neither English nor African, yet somehow both. She would have been equally at home having tea with the queen of England or learning to make a secret healing balm from one of Jamaica's many African herbalists deep in the countryside.

Within weeks I had figured out a key fact: Miss Claire and I were both rebels. But age and loss had brought wisdom to Miss Claire's rebellion, whereas I was always ready to tilt at windmills. If the mythical Don Quixote had ever fathered a daughter, I would have been that daughter, racing off on my horse, wielding a too-short lance, ready to fight Mandeville's high and mighty every time one of them openly disparaged or otherwise mistreated poor or uneducated people in my presence.

For long stretches of time, I must have fought at least one battle a day.

Before I quite realized it, Miss Claire's residence became my second home. There, she listened patiently to my war stories, occasionally asking a gently probing question or two.

"And so, Miss Cynthia ... Do you think there might have been another way to attack that problem?" she might ask as we sipped our tea, minutes after I'd arrived at her home feeling bruised from losing another fight.

It was the perfect approach to take with a girl who was often frustrated by the inequities of Jamaican society and ill equipped to fight them. Instead of giving advice, instead of telling me what I should have done, Miss Claire asked questions that forced me to review the effectiveness of my tactics.

And then, pouring the hot golden liquid into her best china cup, she served me tea – the very elixir most often associated with the very target of my frustration – Mandeville's upper class.

Chapter Eleven

Tempest in a Tea Cup

Miss Claire's opinion mattered a lot, though I wouldn't have admitted it at the time.

Perhaps, deep down, I didn't quite believe that she was as decent as she seemed. Perhaps, when push came to shove, she would slip up and reveal that she was really just another upper-class Mandeville lady like all the rest, with their hats and gloves and tea parties and servants and class prejudices.

One day, I announced to Miss Claire that I planned to invite her gardener to the movies that Saturday. His name was Albert Jones, and he might have been somewhere in his mid-thirties. Miss Claire called him "Mr. Albert" or "Mr. Jones," and I did the same. He was a gentle man.

I fully expected Miss Claire to be impressed, surprised, even shocked by the idea. This was, after all, Mandeville. One did not invite a friend's gardener to the movies.

From the neutral tone of her voice, I might as well have given her news about the weather.

"And why do you want to do that, Miss Cynthia?" she asked, in that deliberate, almost formal way of hers, angling her head to one side and looking more curious than anything else.

"Because I'm disgusted with the way these upper-class people in Mandeville treat the poor uneducated people," I said, with all the self-righteousness I could muster. "They treat their dogs and cats a lot better than the people who work in their homes!"

It was, of course, a gross overstatement against a whole class of people. And with it, I'd just brashly proven myself guilty of the very thing I hated in this town: prejudice.

But Miss Claire didn't bat an eyelash.

"So, Miss Cynthia, you're doing this ... inviting Mr. Jones to the movies ... to make a point about class discrimination here in Mandeville?"

"Yes, I am. And what's wrong with *that?*"

She was utterly unfazed by my outburst.

"And, Miss Cynthia ... Have you given any thought to how that would make Mr. Jones feel? Being seen in public at the movies with a teenage girl who's not a relative?"

I hadn't thought of that. Come to think of it, I didn't have a clue whether Mr. Jones even liked going to the movies. I started to squirm in my seat.

Holding my gaze, Miss Claire went on: "Like it or not, Miss Cynthia ... you're somewhat privileged yourself. Even upper class, compared with Mr. Jones. By going to the movies with him ... in front of all of Mandeville ... you'll make a public spectacle of yourself. And ... much more important ... you'll make a spectacle of *him*."

Continuing in the same reasonable tone, Miss Claire said, "And I suppose that's the point."

I finally found my voice.

"I am *not* privileged," I protested. "And I do *not* belong to the upper class!"

I wasn't lying. But I wasn't telling the whole truth either. Yes, my family was nowhere close to being upper class. But I belonged to a middle-class country family that valued education, and I had excelled in the

British-Jamaican school system. Many Jamaicans were fluent in one language. I spoke three. At the drop of a hat, I could quote Shakespeare, Dickens, Balzac, Molière, Cervantes.

On top of all that, my family had owned land for generations. In the stratified society of Mandeville, all of this meant that I belonged to a quite different economic and social class from Mr. Jones the gardener.

But I was too young, too proud, and by now had invested too much in my rebellion to back down. Raising my voice, I told Miss Claire that my mind was made up. I was going to the movies, and I was inviting Mr. Jones to come with me.

Miss Claire was silent, and for a moment I thought I had won. When she finally spoke, she was more formal than I had ever heard her. I had to lean in to hear.

"You are a guest in my home," she said. "Mr. Jones is employed by me. I will not have him used to make your political point."

She was right, and we both knew it. I would never admit that her calm response had changed my mind, and we both knew that, too. I would not be inviting Mr. Jones to the movies.

~

Miss Claire took tea seriously, for two reasons. First, she loved it. Although she preferred the Chinese oolong and jasmine teas, believing they helped to calm the mind, she catered to the preferences of her guests and always had a variety of teas on hand. Second, she possessed the mysterious talent of reading tealeaves. Visitors came from across the country to have their leaves read by her on her days off from the telephone company. Some were friends of hers, and some were my own friends; she read their tealeaves as a gift. But as her readings became famous for being accurate, her visitors multiplied, and she started to charge a small fee to those who could afford it.

One day, a tall, sophisticated woman whom we'd never met sat down at Miss Claire's dining table for a reading. Miss Claire's unusual mixture of old-fashioned grace and wit charmed her guest immediately as the three of us sat and enjoyed our tea together.

It was a beautiful spring day, the kind of day where clouds of pretty blue forget-me-nots are in full bloom in the garden, the skies are blue and endless, and all seems right with the world.

Inside, the house felt dead silent, fraught with expectation, hope, and a slight undercurrent of apprehension at what the tealeaves would foretell.

I decided to take a stroll in the garden, allowing the two women privacy.

"Please stay," the guest asked, touching my arm as I started to stand.

Looking into her face, I realized that this confident-looking woman with the elegant clothes, long polished fingernails, and glowing brown skin was nervous about the reading. I sat down beside her.

Miss Claire picked up the pretty bone china cup the woman had been drinking from. She angled it to peer at the formation of the leaves inside. Her large almond-shaped eyes were intent, her smooth, unlined face immobile. Finally, she began to speak.

"You've been married for nine years," Miss Claire observed quietly but firmly, looking steadfastly at the tealeaves. "It was a good strong marriage for some years."

The woman nodded vigorously.

Miss Claire paused.

"You recently got pregnant after trying for several years."

Our visitor drew in her breath sharply.

Miss Claire continued, speaking softly.

"You miscarried."

The woman doubled over as though she had received a physical blow. Just as quickly, she straightened up. But she struggled to catch her breath.

Miss Claire paused again, allowing her visitor to regain her dignity before saying, even more softly, "It was a boy."

The visitor reached for my hand and held on to it tightly.

"Things have been very difficult of late."

The woman swayed slightly against me.

"My dear, you ..." Miss Claire began.

I caught the change in her tone, because by now I knew her mannerisms well. Whatever was coming was not good news.

Just then, through the open window, we heard a bird start to sing. It was a most peculiar but beautiful song, and its sweet clarity pierced the silence. In that moment, the house seemed to come alive with warmth and vitality and something that felt like hope.

Almost as distinctively, a second bird replied, picking up the unusual melody. Miss Claire turned her head to look through the window. Her whole body was taut. The visitor turned and stared with her, angling her head toward the sound.

For a long moment, we three women sat transfixed, caught in a still-life painting as two birds sang their magical song.

"Ah," breathed Miss Claire at last, relaxing back into her chair as the birds ended their music. "The birds are singing. It is a sign of hope."

I had heard her perform several readings, usually for my friends or relatives. Never before had I seen her back away from something she had seen so clearly in someone's cup, deciding not to reveal its contents.

Smoothly, Miss Claire returned to the reading, giving a message of hope to a fragile woman.

The guest left with a spring in her step, her power returned to her by a rare session with a rare woman.

~

I dropped in to visit one afternoon a few weeks later. As I sipped tea with Miss Claire, she said, "A little reading of the tealeaves?"

I had steadfastly refused to let Miss Claire read my own tealeaves. She knew so many of my yearnings for the future. I was afraid she would just tell me what I wanted to hear.

On this afternoon, I relented, my curiosity finally getting the better of me.

Miss Claire's reading consisted mostly of small predictions about friends and family. Her biggest revelation was that I would go abroad to study. On that point she was emphatic.

I could hardly allow myself to believe it. Going abroad to study was my fondest wish.

Part Two

Northern Home

*You can never go home again,
but the truth is,
you can never leave home,
so it's all right.*

~ Maya Angelou

Chapter Twelve

Inhaling Ice

My first breath of Canada's winter air was like inhaling ice.

I stood in the exit doorway of Toronto's international airport fighting the urge to run back into the warmth and fly back to Jamaica.

"Welcome to Canada," the sign said.

Welcome, indeed, I thought, my face already starting to freeze.

How could people live in this awful place? I wondered, thanking God I wouldn't have to stay forever. I was here for only a few years, then I'd be going home. I just had to be patient and brave.

And wear very warm clothes.

It hadn't been easy getting this far. The Canadian High Commission in Kingston, Jamaica, had somehow lost my files, but refused to admit it. I had almost given up when, by one of those surprising strokes of luck, I helped a caller to fix his home telephone problem. That caller turned out to be an official at the Canadian High Commission.

In return, he said, "If you ever need my help, please don't be afraid to ask."

So I called him back and asked if he would find out what had become of my application.

One search, one mistake discovered, and one apology later, I had my Canadian immigration papers – providing that I could be in Canada within two weeks. If not, the process would have to start all over again, medical examinations and all.

I had wanted this opportunity with all my heart. But two weeks?

Two weeks to leave my home, my family, and the only country I knew. There was only one way to cope: for those two weeks, I lived in my head, ignoring the emotions that lay just below the surface of my skin.

The fearful pounding of my heart, late at night. The drumbeat of excitement mixed with fear.

I quit the telephone job, packed my suitcases with the warmest clothes I could find, and said goodbye to family and friends.

As the plane climbed into the skies over Jamaica, I thought of my family home, my grandmother's old house, the little pink house with the trees and stream – but most of all, of my parents and siblings. I was the first of the five children to leave Jamaica, and neither I nor they had any idea when we'd see each other again.

I imagined that, way down below the airplane, my father was trying to be stoical, my mother smiling and praying at the same time. Only then did I give in to tears.

But I was determined to hold myself together. I silently chanted a consolation that I would use over and over again in the months ahead: this was only a temporary parting. I'd be away from home for just a few years.

In front of me was a wonderful opportunity to learn, grow up, and get a few years of Canadian work experience. And then I would return to my beloved Jamaica, land of my birth, land of my family.

But first I had to step out into the freezer called Canada and master the art of inhaling ice.

~

I was allowed into Canada as a "nominated relative" of an aunt and uncle who lived in Kitchener-Waterloo, some seventy miles west of Toronto. They were at the airport to meet me, and, as we drove along Highway 401, I was comforted by their overflowing generosity and kindness. It was an awesome gift they were giving me: helping me to emigrate from a faraway island and bringing me to live in their home.

No two ways about it, though. I was no longer at home. Winter in Kitchener-Waterloo meant snowbanks piled high on both sides of the road. When I exhaled, I could see my breath like steam in front of my face. I walked carefully, gingerly, every time I stepped outside. In time I learned to fall less often, and when I did fall, to land without breaking anything important.

It was a great lesson for life.

Once in Kitchener-Waterloo, I applied for a job as a telephone operator and in the interview proved that Jamaica had taught me well. As if guided by an unseen hand, things fell into place. I got the evening shift and enrolled in daytime classes in Canadian studies: history, economics, politics, and French- and English-Canadian literature.

I was on a crash course to learn everything I could about Canada while I tried to gain the knowledge I needed for the next step, my dream: being accepted into Ryerson Polytechnic in Toronto to study magazine journalism. Working and studying full-time was exhausting, but I had come here with a plan, and now I was on my way.

Gratitude filled my heart.

I stopped complaining about the cold.

~

My first hour on the switchboard at Bell Canada proved how little I knew about this new country.

A customer called.

"Operator?"

"Good morning, sir!"

"I wanna call Chranna."

"Yes sir ..."

"Chranna."

"Glad to help, sir."

I guessed that Chranna was a place, not a person.

"Do you have the area code and number?"

"No, I need to make a person-to-person call, and I don't know the number. Would you get it for me?"

As he rattled off the name of the person and the name of the company where she worked, I desperately searched my long-distance handbook. Chranna. Charanna. Tranna ... no such place name.

"Sir, could you spell the name of the place you are calling?"

"Chranna? Operator, are you ... are you ... You don't know how to spell Chranna? You *don't know* Chranna?"

It was the seventies, and telephone operators were all located in the city or region they served. These women – they were almost all women – often knew the names and phone numbers of their callers before they identified themselves. Clearly, there was a Chranna or Tranna lurking somewhere. But where?

My supervisor, Mary, had plugged into the switchboard to monitor my first calls.

"Just ask him to hold on," she whispered.

I could have sworn there were tears in her eyes. Tears she was trying to hide.

This is not a good sign, I thought. Already I had made a big mistake.

"He means To-ron-to," she said, sounding out the syllables after taking a deep breath.

"To-ron-to. Oh! Why didn't he say so? And they think *I* have an accent ..."

I turned back to the switchboard and flipped my key to talk to the customer again. Mary turned her head away. But not before I caught the look on her face.

Those were tears of laughter that she'd been trying to hide.

That first year in Kitchener-Waterloo, whenever I pulled on my headset and plugged into the Bell switchboard, I learned about the place names of the region, the country, and the outside world. That's how I first got to know the country: through its telephone system.

~

Life has its ironies. While I could call anywhere in the world from my position on the switchboard, there was one place I constantly longed to call but couldn't. Home.

I missed the warmth, the sunshine, the mountain breeze, the scent of flowers, the people. Most of all, I missed my family. But, living on the mountainside, my parents didn't have a telephone. So my mother and I had to settle for writing long letters, each one arriving in the mail like a priceless gem. That's how I discovered, for the first time, that my mother was an excellent writer. And a comedian. Some of her letters – describing the antics of beloved family members, neighbours, people at church – made me laugh out loud.

I was discovering a lot of new things, often by trial and error. But perhaps the most important thing was getting the slang right, as I learned the first time I went to a hair salon.

"What would you like to get done?" asked the young woman in the tight black pants and colourful top.

"I just want to get my hair washed, trimmed, and dried," I answered cheerfully. "Not a curl job. Just a blow job."

As the young woman stared at me in astonishment, I stared back, blithely unaware of my huge gaffe. Alarm didn't register till, job completed and paid for, she handed me my change.

"Um ... you know ..."

"Yes?"

I smiled brightly to encourage her.

"Well, it's just that – don't *ever* use that word again! It's called a 'blow dry.' The other thing is completely different ..."

I was mortified when someone later explained that a blow job was a sexual act.

I discovered that Canadians have a dry sense of humour. For months, both at work and at school, I found myself taking people's words far too seriously, failing to recognize subtlety or ironic intent. For a time, after catching on to this, I smiled or laughed at everything anyone said. I stopped after realizing that a co-worker's father really had fallen down dead at the dining table, head first in his soup. So I decided on a far safer route. I used a stock response to everything that was said to me: "Oh, really! That's interesting."

I never laughed or sympathized until a real Canadian had done so first.

Many people ended their sentences with an "eh" – a cross between a word and an inflection with a multitude of roles. Storytelling was one of them.

"So, we're driving along the road, eh? And then out of nowhere, a deer crosses the road, eh?"

This "eh," I learned, stood in for "you see?"

"Eh" could also mean, "Am I right in thinking this?" As in, "You're leaving now, eh?"

But a simple "eh?" uttered in isolation could also mean: "Say that again?" or "What do you mean?"

All very confusing for a girl from Jamaica.

I noticed, however, that well-educated Canadians rarely used the "eh," reacting to it the way some people look down their noses at someone slurping soup. I vowed that I wouldn't use it either.

How was I to know that the Canadian "eh" can creep up on a person unawares?

On a trip to California years later, a woman I had just met kept asking me questions. Only later would I realize that she wasn't particularly interested in what I said, but delighted in my Canadian accent, particularly my use of the expression "eh." Not only had I assimilated the "eh" into my speech, I had also adopted the Canadian "hoose" for house, "a-boot" for about, and "oot" for out.

You could have knocked me down with a Canada goose feather.

~

A good education back in Jamaica, high grades, and, by now, some life experience got me into the prestigious journalism school at Ryerson Polytechnic where I would learn the importance of other words such as "who, what, when, where, why, and how," all key questions for a journalist.

My big ambition was to write feature articles for magazines. But by the time I got to the registration desk, that class was full. Only one course still had space. Television journalism. So I signed up.

But I still needed to work, to pay the bills. With great references from my switchboard supervisors Mary and Marion in Kitchener-Waterloo, I lucked into a job at Bell Canada in downtown Toronto, a short walk from Ryerson. I had learned French and Spanish at high school, which made me one of a tiny group of Bell's multilingual telephone operators. And by now I'd pretty well mastered the Canadian accent so had no trouble understanding place names on the phone.

I went to school during the day and worked the switchboard at night. I had no social life. None.

But it seemed I had a talent for television journalism.

Recruiters for the Canadian Broadcasting Corporation, Canada's largest and most esteemed broadcaster, were on their annual swing across Canada, interviewing top students at each of the journalism schools. They came to Ryerson, interviewed candidates, and chose me for their national TV News summer apprenticeship program.

My journalism professor tried to change their minds, arguing that this incredible opportunity should go to a real Canadian. What he never bothered to ask me was whether I intended to stay in Canada or return to Jamaica. Because by then I not only had decided to become a Canadian but also had made a sacred pledge: my oath of Canadian citizenship.

All the while, homesickness was a constant low-grade ache in my gut. I missed family and friends. The mountains and the beaches. The sun and the food and the rhythms of Jamaica.

But there was no longer any real question of going back home. As much as I missed my homeland, if I stayed in Canada I would live in a far bigger, wider, more challenging world. With many more opportunities.

Chapter Thirteen

A Good Time

And so it was that, fresh out of journalism school, I became a trainee reporter in the CBC's TV News summer trainee program in Toronto. It was a great honour, awarded to only six journalism graduates from all the J-schools in the country. After a few weeks' intensive training, most of us would be shipped off to various cities across the country for the four months of late spring and summer. One would stay in Toronto.

I begged the CBC executives to let me be that one. Toronto had become my home city. Or at least to send me to romantic Montreal, where I could use my French. But the CBC brass had other ideas.

"You need to develop a sense of Canada," they pointed out, "especially since you are an immigrant."

So they sent me as far away as possible. To Vancouver.

Going to faraway places didn't frighten me. After all, only a few years earlier, I'd left my homeland on two weeks' notice and come to Canada to live. But Vancouver's reputation, despite its vaunted natural charms, was not encouraging.

"In Vancouver, they're laid back to the point of being comatose!" a senior journalist in Toronto warned. "And they're not nice to people from the east!"

Even worse, CBC TV in Vancouver had a scary history with young summer trainee journalists sent from Toronto. Seems the newsroom liked to eat them alive.

What would they make of me in Vancouver? I was from the east. Worse, I was a walking advertisement for everything rare in Canadian newsrooms: brown skin, a Spanish last name, traces of a Jamaican accent at a time when English-Canadian newsrooms barely tolerated a French-Canadian or Newfoundland accent on the air. I was also a young woman.

As I packed my suitcase and prepared to head west, my emotions swung between gung-ho determination and total fear.

I arrived in Vancouver, checked in at the YWCA's hostel downtown, freshened up, and mulled over all that advice from the CBC Training Department. Get to know the city as quickly as possible, they had told me. Go walk about. Meet people. Ask questions.

No time like the present, I thought.

So, wearing no makeup, hair pulled back in a ponytail, I went out to learn about Vancouver. I had gone barely a block when a handsome, clean-cut young man wearing tennis gear and carrying a racquet sauntered up to me.

"Wanna have a good time?" he asked with a friendly smile.

"What do you mean – have a good time? What? Where?"

"Wherever you want. My place isn't too far away. How much?"

"How much what?"

"How much do you charge?"

"For what?"

"A good time."

Comprehension dawned on both of us at the same time. Suddenly the young man was blushing, stammering, apologizing profusely.

"I'm a TV news reporter," I said sternly, the first time I'd been able to say those words. They sounded marvellous.

I might as well have said I was a police officer. The young man bolted, leaving me gaping after him. I wasn't sure which surprised me more: his mistaking me for a prostitute, or that a clean-cut young man would try to buy sex on the way home from his tennis game. Who knew that tennis was such an aphrodisiac?

I finally burst out laughing. At myself.

Vancouver is delightful if you don't mind the frequent rain. It's an easy city to fall in love with, blessed by majestic mountains, a mighty ocean, and the outstanding beauty of Stanley Park, a forest right in the city. In Vancouver, you can hike, ski, and sail, all on the same day.

I lucked out on the sailing. Within a day I found an apartment and a roommate who sailed on weekends. In practically no time I was learning to sail on the Pacific Ocean. I felt strong, adventurous, ready to take on the world.

And then I arrived at the newsroom for my first day of work.

All that confidence from learning to sail a boat, all that sense of importance I felt when I told the tennis player I was a TV news reporter, vanished when I arrived there and learned that I was neither expected nor needed in the newsroom. A very slightly apologetic editor broke that news to me.

In one fell swoop, I felt discarded, and in a strange way, entirely homeless. But I couldn't leave. Too much was riding on this spring and summer.

Finally, after a frantic call to Toronto, I won a reprieve. The Vancouver newsroom bosses told me I could stay. But there was neither a desk nor a phone for me to use at that time.

I was on my own.

Chapter Fourteen

Mountain Cabin

With no one to care about how I spent my time, I wandered the city looking for a story, any story, hoping to impress the assignment editor and buy myself a chance to practice my new profession.

But how on earth do you do that when you're a stranger?

I walked down one unfamiliar street, up another. I tried to talk to people waiting at bus stops or sitting in cafés. But this was Vancouver, not my Jamaican hometown, where if you *didn't* stop to talk you were considered very rude.

Then, in a small clothing store, I hit pay dirt. When I entered, a petite, strikingly good-looking elderly woman, her black hair pulled back into an elegant chignon, greeted me and invited me to look around. Her tone was friendly, and her smile seemed genuine. Before long, we chose a dress for me to try on.

I opened the door of the change room and started to undress when my eyes caught the scene around me. It was like entering the wardrobe in the Narnia Chronicles and finding oneself in a strange and beautiful world. Every wall was covered with photographs of ballet dancers, most of them autographed. Rudolf Nureyev, Margot Fonteyn, Vaslav Nijinksy, Anna Pavlova, and many others, famous or merely beautiful, were captured in full performance or just smiling into the lens.

I half-opened the door of the change room and called out, "Why do you have all these photos of dancers on your walls?"

"They're people I danced with," the woman said easily. "Some were my friends. A few were just great dancers whom I admired."

Closing the door, I took another look at the photos and noticed this time that several of them portrayed a young dancer who looked strangely familiar. Then, as I emerged from the change room, it hit me. The beautiful young woman in the classical bell tutu and ballet slippers was the younger version of the woman now standing in front of me.

"Please tell me about yourself and your dance friends," I pleaded.

An hour later, I bought myself a new dress. Even better, I got myself a story.

A few days later, the CBC's supper-hour news carried the story of a seventy-five-year-old Vancouver woman who had danced with some of the world's greatest ballet companies alongside dancers whose names were part of the ballet world's history. Now, out of the glare of the spotlight, she ran a tiny store that sold ladies' fashions and dance costumes.

She also taught ballet. Our television camera followed her graceful movements. Behind her, albeit less gracefully, the boys and girls in her class followed her moves.

Adagio, arabesque, battement, jeté, pas de deux, entrechat.

Her love of music and dance was so powerful, it radiated from her in great yearning waves of beauty and lit up the television screen. All edited to the music of Debussy's sad, magical *Clair de Lune*.

The story was a hit with the viewers. But in the news-room, I was still persona non grata.

Every weekday morning I walked from my shared apartment in the west end of the city to the CBC building downtown, taking the same route home in the evening. The walk was pleasant, partly because of my friendly chit-chats with a trio of elegant women who stood in front of a prestigious hotel, apparently waiting for rides home. These friendly, articulate, cheerful women and my room-mate were my only friends in the city for much of my time there.

But lacking friends didn't particularly worry me. I was in Vancouver to make a career, not friends. I hit the ground running, finding and reporting on two, sometimes three news stories a day. My unrelenting work ethic, and a fierce desire to get the facts of a story right, paid off. I finally won over even the supervisor who had told me, that first day in the newsroom, to go back home to Toronto. And I got my own desk and phone: my own little patch of home in a big impersonal newsroom.

I learned that I had something more than just a good journalistic work ethic going for me. Outside the news-room, people found me unthreatening, even naïve. This, coupled with my newness to the city, sometimes led total strangers, despite the TV camera looming behind me, to answer my unsophisticated questions with unusual candour.

But that same lack of sophistication nearly did me in.

Someone in the CBC newsroom had a friend who was about to set off on a cross-Canada trip with his wife and needed a house sitter for his log cabin on a mountainside lot overlooking Vancouver. A log cabin! You couldn't get any more homey and Canadian than living in a log cabin. I went to meet the owners.

The cabin was perfect. Tucked into the forest, built of

dark-stained logs, it looked a natural part of the mountain that towered above it. The tiny house was simple but comfortable, warm and unpretentious. Its floors and simple furnishings were flooded with light from large, uncovered windows. Except for the bathroom, every room in the house was small – which made the house only more appealing. I liked small houses.

I settled up with my roommate, packed my few belongings into the cabin owners' car, which had been left behind for my use, and headed up the mountain. For the first time since arriving in this city, I felt comfortable.

I was in Vancouver, where it was easy to buy fresh salmon, fresh asparagus, fresh berries, fresh everything. Driving home from work – even though I had to battle the notorious rush-hour traffic on the Lions Gate Bridge – was a joy. I could hardly wait to pull into the driveway, turn the key in the lock of the front door, kick off my shoes, and head to the kitchen to try my hand at cooking west coast salmon.

This small house was my refuge from the newsroom, and I gave thanks for it daily.

To make my happiness even more complete, my only responsibilities were to keep the house clean and water the many vigorous-looking houseplants. As I cleaned and watered, I prayed fervently that the plants would stay alive, at least until their owners returned.

Late one night, weeks after I moved in, the sound of sawing woke me. Who on earth would be sawing logs at this time of night? As I listened more closely, it sounded as though the person was sawing the cabin itself. For the first time in this cabin in the woods, I felt vulnerable. I was alone. Suddenly, the huge, uncovered windows scared me. Whoever was out there could see clearly in.

On hands and knees I crawled across the floor to the telephone in the living room and called the police. The

Royal Canadian Mounted Police dispatcher promised to get an officer to the cabin as soon as possible. I waited, fighting panic.

The two officers who showed up were young, fresh-faced, and friendly. They looked around for signs of an intruder and searched the surrounding trees with powerful flashlights. Again and again they asked me to describe exactly what I had heard.

"It was probably a bear," the male officer concluded. "You're in the mountain, and they come down at night sometimes. I think the sound you heard was likely a bear scratching on logs. Not someone sawing."

They decided to check the inside of the house, just in case. I huddled in my bathrobe on the sofa, still unnerved by it all.

They returned to the living room together.

"Nice plants you have growing in the bathroom," said the male officer.

Idiots! I thought. *This is no time to be admiring house-plants.* But I simply nodded agreement.

"They're growing really nicely," said the female officer.

I wanted to kick them, or at least scream out loud.

Be nice, I told myself wearily. *They came all this way. They've been polite. They just really seem to like plants.*

"Yes," I said aloud, trying to sound as though I shared their avid interest in houseplants. "It's a large bathroom, lots of glass. No curtains and great sunlight in the daytime. That must be what makes them so healthy, because all I do is water them."

The two police officers glanced at each other. I could swear they were sharing a secret joke. Then they left, telling me to call if I heard the sound again.

I went back to bed, still shaken, and now suspicious of the police officers. Had they concluded that I was just another crazy woman who had overreacted to the sounds of the mountain? Or even made the whole thing up?

When the homeowners returned from their cross-country tour, they were delighted that I had taken such excellent care of their house. Then I told them about the night the police visited and searched the rooms.

"They were in the bathroom for a long time, admiring your plants."

"They *what*?"

"It really bugged me at the time, because they kept going on about how healthy the plants were, while I was still shaking with fear over what I thought was a prowler or a burglar."

There was a long, strange pause.

Finally the woman said, so softly I could hardly hear her, "Cynthia, we thought you knew."

"Knew what?"

"Well, you said you were originally from Jamaica."

"Yeaaahhh ...?"

"Well, we thought you knew ... we thought you would know ... what those plants are."

She looked at me as though she was seeing me for the first time.

"What are they? And what does Jamaica have to do with it?"

"Cynthia, those are marijuana plants," the husband said, as though explaining a simple concept to a hopeless idiot.

"Mari – *who*? You mean ... as in Ganja? Weed? *That* marijuana?"

"Yes."

"Did you tell the cops when we were coming back?" the wife asked anxiously.

I couldn't remember.

Staring at them, I didn't know which revelation shocked me more. That I had spent the summer diligently caring for a marijuana crop, or that two such respectable-looking people grew marijuana plants in their house and had assumed that I knew – simply because I'd been brought up in Jamaica.

What, I wondered, would my mother say if she could see me now?

Gathering my wits, I explained a simple fact to my hosts. That many Jamaicans had never seen ganja, except perhaps on TV. For obvious reasons, the illegal plant was grown in secret places, usually far away from people and neighbourhoods.

The couple decided to get rid of the plants right away.

~

By the time the summer ended, I had sharpened my skills. I observed everything and everyone more carefully, and checked everything twice. It had been a gruelling summer, but I felt I had accomplished a lot. I had broken important stories on CBC Vancouver's evening news and received job offers from news directors in other cities who had seen my stories on the satellite feeds.

I was finally a real journalist and proud of it.

But as my mother once told me, just as you get too full of yourself, life conspires to keep you grounded by delivering a small banana peel for you to slip on.

It was late afternoon, the end of my last shift. The cameraman was driving the soundman and me back to the newsroom. Along the way, we passed the three women who had been so friendly at the beginning of summer. There they were, standing in their usual spot in front of the hotel. I asked the cameraman to stop for a moment. Hugging each woman a warm goodbye, I thanked them for their encouragement and support through my early months in their city.

The crewmen were strangely silent when I got back in the car.

Minutes later, one of them asked, "Cynthia – how do you know those women?"

"From my walks home from work earlier in the summer. They were very nice, friendly, very helpful to me. Told me about shops and hairdressers when I really didn't know anybody."

For a few minutes, no one spoke.

"Cynthia – do you know what these women do for a living?" the soundman asked.

I was puzzled by the question, but emphatic in my answer.

"Oh yes," I said. "They work at the hotel. I saw them every evening waiting for their husbands to pick them up."

The cameraman cleared his throat and touched my arm.

"You may be right about where they work, Cynthia, but not about what they do. Well ... not exactly. Those women are hookers. And the men they're waiting for aren't their husbands."

I stared at the two men, wanting to ask how they knew this with such certainty, wondering if they were pulling my leg. But they were colleagues I had come to respect, and I could see they weren't joking.

Still, how could such cheerful, elegant, smart, and friendly women possibly be hookers?

"OK, turn around! Let's go back." I said. "I have to find out if that's true."

But by the time we reached the hotel, all three were gone.

"Well, hookers or not, they are *still* very nice women," I said. I thought about it. "It figures," I said, groaning in mock despair. "The first person who warmly greeted me in this city thought *I* was a hooker. Virtually the only people who befriended me were hookers. Oh, wow!"

By now we were all hooting with laughter.

Chapter Fifteen

Enter, Hamlin

"Think I'll ever get married like you, with a home and family of my own, Mama?"

For almost as long as I could remember, I asked my mother this question at least once a year.

"If that is what God wants for you, you surely will," she always replied.

I figured she was hedging her bets.

As I grew older, Mama always gave me a mysterious smile before replying. Then one day she came right out with it: "You will, but he's going to have to be a very special person."

"W-what?" I replied, laughing. "Are you saying I'm such a difficult personality that nobody would want to marry me? Or is this just because I refuse to cook?"

Now we were both giggling, and my mother gave a different answer this time.

"I'm saying if you decide to be a rebel for the rest of your life, the least you should do is learn how to cook!"

"I'm going to find me a man who can cook," I said. "Somebody has to, or I'll die of starvation!"

When I moved to Canada, my mother and I often communicated in our letters by teasing each other. Truth was, though, I came to value her advice more and more.

So when I finally met a man I thought I could settle down with, I sent him to meet my parents. His name was Hamlin, and he happened to be visiting Jamaica on business. I asked him to drive to Manchester and see my folks at the family home.

"What did my mother say?" I asked anxiously when he returned to Canada.

"She told me to run fast in the opposite direction," was all he said.

I couldn't stand the suspense.

"What did she say?" I asked again.

It turns out that, when my mother met Hamlin and heard how he felt about me, she smiled, looked him in the eye, and said, "That one is a rebel. Do you know that?"

"My mother said that?" I asked, not quite believing it and yet knowing it to be true.

"That's exactly what she said." Then, after a pause, he added, "She also said you are kind, honest, intelligent, and very brave."

"Well, thank God for that," I said, with both sarcasm and relief.

But Hamlin was determined to keep teasing me.

"What's a man to think when a woman's own mother warns him off about her daughter?" he asked, laughter in his eyes.

"That she's a rebel," I replied, grinning now. "Can't say you haven't been warned!"

Despite the warning, Hamlin and I moved in together. There was no doubt who had the better culinary skills. He knew how to cook and enjoyed doing it. I, meanwhile, cooked for the sole purpose of stopping hunger. Perhaps it was seeing my mother slaving over the proverbial hot stove day after day during my childhood that had put me off cooking. Except for my brief time in the log cabin – where I happily steamed asparagus, boiled potatoes, and pan-fried salmon steaks every day for dinner – cooking had never held any appeal for me.

I considered myself very lucky to have met Hamlin. Here was a smart man, a funny man, an athletic man, a man who loved books and cooking, worked as a journalist, and – wonder of wonders – had lived only about two miles from my childhood home back when we were both six. We had gone to different schools and had never met each other.

"You were practically the boy next door!" I said.

One day I slipped Hamlin a note, asking him to marry me. He let me wait for several hours, pretending he hadn't seen the note. So I went about my business, pretending it had never happened. And then he said yes, with a mischievous laugh.

I groaned and rolled my eyes, and then we both laughed. It wasn't the most romantic proposal or acceptance, and the woman had popped the question. But it was uniquely ours. As was the wedding that followed shortly after. Our vows were blessed by our priest in a tiny chapel, and dinner was at the home of a friend. It was small, it was inexpensive, it was different, and it was ours.

Chapter Sixteen

The Red Brick House

Every young couple dreams of buying a home together. So it was with Hamlin and me.

Over several years, we rented. First the house that froze during winter, no matter how much heat we pumped in. We should have known it wouldn't turn out well when, weeks after we moved in, the driveway almost ate our car. We watched it sink into the gravel to its hubcaps, not knowing if it would stop.

Then there was the house with the flooded basement. When the water receded, we had a new houseguest: an enormous rat.

That settled it. By now, the early eighties, we had a sweet little daughter, Nikisha, and more than ever we wanted a warm – and *safe* – house. But, we admitted to ourselves, it also had to be charming. Over and over, we used the same word. Charming.

The word meant roughly the same to both of us. A place that would feel like home. A place we'd be proud to come home to. With a landscaped front garden, heavy with trees, bushes, and flowers. A grassy back yard, big enough for our daughter to play in, wide enough for a vegetable garden. French doors. A fireplace. Wood trim around windows and doorways.

We could see it, feel it, smell it, touch it. Our first house. Charming.

Harry, our real estate agent, showed us dozens of houses that oozed charm. Our hearts filled with joy as we imagined ourselves living graciously in these lovely houses with their gleaming wood staircases and floors and large sunlit kitchens.

It took very little time to discover the sobering truth. Any house that charming and not out of our financial league had serious flaws. A leaky roof. Seriously sloping floors. A damp, mouldy basement. Flimsy structural supports. One house even had obvious signs of termites.

But we were obsessed with charm. We were determined to find the house of our dreams. So Harry shrugged and dutifully took us to inspect one charming house after another.

Harry was around seventy, a man who had lived in Ontario all his life and been a real estate agent for much of it. He had a prominent nose and steady eyes that seemed to say *nothing surprises me anymore.*

He had a strong sense of style: solid, reliable, and thoroughly out of fashion. Every day he wore the same old brown coat and matching, shapeless hat and a version of the same polyester brown trousers, plaid shirt, and sensible black galoshes over brown shoes. All of them seemed roughly the same vintage as his car, a battered brown and beige station wagon with seats littered with real estate pamphlets, a large flashlight, and a measuring tape.

One day, when we'd fallen in and out of love with a charming century-old cottage with a roof that leaked and plaster walls with huge cracks, Harry fixed us with a steady gaze through his large horn-rimmed glasses. In a voice like crushed gravel, he tried to bring us to our senses.

"You know that place you saw in the real estate

flyer? The one you want to look at next?" he asked. "It looks great, right? All dolled up like?" He smiled. "All 'charming'?"

We nodded eagerly, anxious to get going, to finally see this dream house.

"I went to check on it last evening," Harry said, his voice taking on a no-nonsense tone. "Needs an entirely new roof. Basement damp. Floors wonky. It's no good."

He took charge. This time, he said, he was taking us to see a house that felt right for a young family that was "just starting out." He walked off toward his old brown and beige station wagon. We followed meekly.

The house was a narrow, dark-red, two-storey brick building on a quiet street in the east end of Toronto. Almost no front garden. If there was charm here, it seemed to be hiding. But it did have wood floors in living and dining rooms and wood trim around windows and doors. Harry left us to wander around the three modest bedrooms and even more modest bathroom upstairs, while he went off to check out the things that really mattered. He inspected the attic and basement, shone his big flashlight into dark spaces, knocked on interior walls, pulled up the corners of carpets to inspect the flooring underneath.

Finally, he beamed at us like a proud papa.

"We've found your house," he declared. "Roof's good, wiring and plumbing good, drainage good. A solid house. You can live in this house for years and not worry. There'll be only basic maintenance to do. Pay down the mortgage, save some money, then make a few improvements, bit by bit."

It had taken a long time for us to learn this simple fact: we knew nothing about houses. But, somehow, we had ended up in the hands of a master. The offer went in and was accepted.

Months later, husband, wife, and young daughter

moved in, helped by friends and relatives. Not that there was a lot to move at that stage of our lives. The most valuable furniture in the whole house was to be found in our daughter's bedroom: a cream-coloured canopy bed with matching dresser and bookcase. Everything else was either second-hand or just very tired.

And yet, we could barely contain our joy. After years of renting other people's apartments and houses, we finally had our own house. Bit by bit, we told each other, we would paint the walls and change the carpets and even knock down a wall to make the kitchen larger. One day, we might get a dishwasher, a new fridge, or even new cabinets.

One day, when we had money.

Chapter Seventeen

Have House, Will Garden

The land behind the house was almost as thin as the house itself, but it was a long thinness, spread over two terraced levels. We could finally have our own garden. It was something we could do by ourselves, something that was affordable.

All winter long we dreamed. When the birds started to sing, we began the garden drawings in earnest.

What did I think of a garden bed here, another one over there, and railway ties to separate them? Hamlin asked.

How about a bit of lawn over here, a bit of lawn over there? I asked. And wouldn't seeding be cheaper than sodding?

We agreed on everything and returned to dreaming. Husband went to bed and dreamed of tomatoes, lettuce, and corn. Wife went to bed and dreamed of nasturtiums, dahlias, and roses. And as many couples do, we forgot to tell each other exactly what we were dreaming about.

The first doubts didn't come till the first tulip, planted the autumn we moved in, poked its head out of the soil in a corner of the front yard. I had never planted bulbs before, never seen one I'd planted emerge the next spring.

Thrilled at this new life that I had started, I ran back inside the house.

"Come see! Come see!" I yelled.

I practically pulled my fellow gardener, still in his house robe and pyjamas, coffee mug in hand, out of the house to see the miracle.

His lack of excitement could have frozen the tulip's fledgling leaves.

"*This* is what you dragged me out of the house so early in the morning to see?" he asked.

Indeed, it was just after six a.m.

"A tulip popping out of the ground? They have a way of doing that, you know."

How to explain to this Canadian-raised man that he was looking at a genuine miracle? How to explain that in my small mountain village, in the tiny garden bed beneath a front bedroom window of our grandmother's house, a similar miracle had mysteriously taken place every year and was unfolding in our very own garden, right in front of us?

But Hamlin, who had obviously seen spring bulbs come to life every year, was not impressed with my miracle. I watched his back as it disappeared into the house and could practically feel the shrug he shrugged.

Then, just a few weeks later, I was upstairs in the bathroom brushing my teeth when an excited voice cried out: "Atta boy! You finally did it! You finally did it, you little buggers!"

Something was up, but what? I ran down the stairs, toothbrush still in hand.

Standing by the kitchen window was a grown man, leaning over a huge flowerpot with a smile of pure joy on his face.

"They finally did it!"

"Who did what?"

"The peas!" Hamlin yelled, pointing at the potting soil in the flowerpot, with a look that said, "Are you blind or what?"

On closer inspection, I could barely make out little dots of green poking their heads out of the potted soil.

"Hmmm ..." I tried really hard to sound enthusiastic.

Luckily, Nikisha came into the room, caught sight of the little green dots, and rushed to inspect them. Her brown eyes lit up with all the wonder of a small child watching magic.

In no time at all, the garden drawings were put into action. The soil was worked, beds marked, dividers put in place. Soon it would be the May 24 holiday weekend, the time when people in Toronto plant their gardens, hoping that hard frosts were finally behind them.

I could see the garden now: one, maybe two beds for vegetables, and the rest – nothing but beautiful flowers. Lilies, gladioli, sweet alyssum, nasturtiums ... Mmm ... I could practically smell them.

Early in May, a friend gave me a first gift for the garden: peony plants, which bloom big, rose-like pink flowers. Fragrant flowers. I hurried home to plant them in the largest garden bed. With that act, our garden was born. It was time to rejoice.

A few hours later, I was accosted in the kitchen by a madman.

"Did you plant flowers in my bed?" he roared.

Surprised at the question, I forced myself to answer calmly.

"Oh, you mean the peonies? Sure. I planted a few in the large bed on the right."

It was the garden bed that got the best sun.

"But that's the bed I plan to put the tomatoes in!" he half snarled, half wailed. "I spent hours preparing that bed!"

In the briefest of pauses, I tried to think up a reason-able solution. He didn't wait for it.

"I don't want any flowers in that part of the garden," he declared. "Plant them elsewhere!"

I told myself, *you must remember that this man loves you; he's shown it in countless ways.* But the man I loved – the sweet, sensible, decent man I had fallen in love with years earlier – had disappeared, and the alien creature in front of me had just declared war. I took a deep breath and counted to ten before speaking. It didn't work. My temper got the better of me.

"What do you mean?" I shouted. "This house belongs to both of us. Same goes for the garden. You can't tell me where to plant my flowers!"

Hamlin hesitated for just a moment; his voice, when it came, was too measured, too calm.

"Can you eat flowers?" he asked, looking me straight in the eye.

It was a low blow. Even had I known back then that nasturtium flowers *are* edible, these words still would have had their effect. I tried harder, forcing myself to be calm and mature while bizarre and increasingly dire thoughts were beginning to run through my mind.

How could I tell my mother we were getting a divorce over our first garden? And what would we say to Harry, who was still inordinately happy that he had helped a young couple find their perfect home for "starting out"? Harry had been so thrilled that he had come to visit repeatedly, nodding approvingly at the emerging garden.

We glared at each other.

In the pause that hung in the air, my fellow gardener took a deep breath.

"Listen," he said soothingly. "I'll dig some beds closer to the back of the house. That area also gets good sun. You can plant your flowers there."

"But the earth isn't as rich as the soil in those other beds," I said, not ready to give in.

"It is, it is. That's where the yellow tulips are now, and they're doing well, aren't they?"

Very reluctantly, I had to admit this was true.

That Saturday, we visited the garden centre. He headed straight for the little green plants that would later bear veggies. I headed for the little green plants that would bloom beautiful, colourful, fragrant blooms.

He decided to try romaine lettuce. I decided to try cleomes. He reached for a packet of basil seeds. I reached for a dozen gladiolus bulbs.

We paid for our purchases individually and met each other in the doorway.

"What's all that?" we both asked at the same time.

Before he could answer, I was overcome by the urge to challenge.

"Why on earth are you buying romaine lettuce?" I said. "We rarely ever eat the stuff!"

"The same reason you're buying ..." he reached over and pulled a packet of seeds from my black plastic garden centre tray ... "clomies."

Clomies, he called them.

We stared at each other, moved out of the way to let other shoppers pass, looked at each other again. And laughed.

"Come on," I said at last. "Flowers are good for the spirit."

He didn't have to say it. I knew what he was thinking: flowers are good for the spirit, but vegetables are good for the stomach.

We learned to garden together. Slowly at first. Compromising here, giving way there, throwing a fit now and then, always making up before long. In time, I had to admit that his rows of vegetables and herbs were healthy looking and, at harvest time, very edible. He finally admitted that the sight of my flowers did something for his soul.

Through the creation of this garden, we were learning how to live together, solve problems together, and build the foundation for a marriage. The garden became a happy place for our young daughter and us and for relatives and friends who visited.

The house itself improved over time. Slowly, at first. Walls were painted, old carpets ripped up, wood floors sanded. Years later, we finally revived the kitchen with a new dishwasher and fridge, new floors and cupboards.

As house and garden flourished, so did our family.

For our daughter, Nikisha, it was the place of many firsts. It was here that she lost her first baby teeth and grew the first permanent ones. Here that she got her first pets, two goldfish named Cleo and Edgar and a dog named Sprocket. Here that she got her first little patch of earth, planted flower seeds in it, and watched the plants grow. And it was here that she finally got what she wanted most of all: a baby sister.

Our second daughter, Lauren, spent the first three years of her life in this house and garden.

And I learned to cook, sort of. For a while I nurtured the hope that my cooking skills would greatly improve once I had children to cook for. Lord knows I tried. But my efforts to make fabulous meals were as disastrous as my attempts to make cookies for the bake sale at Nikisha's school. As I stared, dumbfounded, at the outcome of my earnest efforts, the children and Hamlin took turns consoling me and giggling.

Since Hamlin was a far better cook, I left the fine cuisine entirely to him, and the children and I looked forward to his exotic dishes on the weekend. I settled down to producing simple weekday meals: honey-mustard chicken, curried shrimp, stir-fries, and other dishes that my family liked, or at least said they did.

Hamlin, meanwhile, discovered he had yet another talent: making up bedtime stories featuring characters that the girls themselves dreamed up. Fastidious lions, cowardly dragons, witches who drove fast sports cars, and a host of other bizarre characters visited the girls' bedrooms every evening, greeted by squeals of laughter and surprise.

The dreams of fancy renovations took a back seat to raising our daughters. "Charm is overrated," we said to each other knowingly, feeling a tiny bit guilty whenever we thought about what we had put dear old Harry through in the early months of our house-hunt.

After several years, we would hit a housing boom, sell our first house at a big profit, and move on, leaving small bits of ourselves behind.

Over the following decade, we would return to the old neighbourhood on several occasions, slowing down in front of our old house each time at the children's request, but never stopping. For several long minutes, memories from our lives in that house would fill the car, along with laughter and the occasional tear.

Harry had been right about this place when he called it "the perfect house for a family just starting out."

What none of us knew was that, many years later, this house would make a miraculous reappearance in our lives.

Chapter Eighteen

Jamaican Dreams

With each passing year, I became less and less Jamaican and more Canadian.

That made sense. I was a Canadian citizen. My husband and daughters were Canadian. Canada was home – had been for nearly fifteen years by now.

That was how I saw my life, most of the time. But the past had a way of tripping me up.

One night, while we were still living in the red brick house that Harry found, I had a dream that all my teeth had fallen out.

My friend Dale, born and raised in Canada, blamed my dream on indigestion.

"Upset stomach," she declared confidently. "Gives you nightmares."

Hamlin, also raised in Canada, had a simpler, more Canadian explanation: "You forgot to brush your teeth before going to bed. That's what your subconscious was trying to tell you."

I laughed and didn't tell him that since I learned as a little girl what a toothbrush was for, I had never forgotten to brush my teeth before bed. Still, unease gnawed at me. I called Pat, my older sister, who had moved to Toronto with her family several years before. She had managed to become Canadian without rejecting Jamaican traditions, cures, and dream interpretations. I knew I could rely on her.

"I dreamed my teeth fell out," I said, trying to keep the anxiety out of my voice.

"Uh-oh," she said. "You know what that means, don't you? Death ..."

"Well, I know it means death if you live in Jamaica. But does it mean the same thing if you live in Canada?" I made a feeble attempt at a laugh, but she didn't laugh back.

As I hung up, I reminded myself that the last time my sister dreamed about fish, no one she knew had gotten pregnant, in direct contradiction of another Jamaican belief.

I tried to forget my dream, but my mind kept shifting gears on its own. I called my sister back.

"Have you heard from home?" I asked.

"Not since Mama phoned three weeks ago. She sounded great and said everyone was fine. Try not to worry yourself."

If I was as Canadian as I claimed, if I had dismissed those Jamaican beliefs as silly superstition, I would have dropped the whole thing there and then.

But I didn't.

As I folded the laundry, another thought popped into my head. Why had our mother phoned? In all the years I'd lived in Canada, she'd only phoned me once. It was the day she got the news that I was pregnant with my first child. Although "the new house" they'd built was only a few miles from Mandeville, my parents still didn't have a telephone because the telephone company said it wasn't "economically feasible" to run a line that far from town.

So why had she travelled to town three weeks ago to call my sister – right after trying to call me? Just to say "hello, everything's fine"? Or had she, too, been dreaming of death?

Maybe the fates were telling me it was time to go home. But then came the automatic reply. I simply couldn't afford the airfare.

It was true. It had just cost a thousand dollars to fix the car. The insurance was due. And they really needed me at work.

It never occurred to me to pay for a flight with my credit card. I had grown up in a rural village where no one ever used a credit card and few people even had a mortgage on their homes. Debt terrified me. A friend diagnosed this as part of the immigrant condition.

"You just don't feel secure enough in this country to go into debt," she said.

"Nonsense," I replied. "I took out a mortgage. That's a lot of debt."

But it just didn't feel right to spend my small savings to fly home.

～

Another memory kept creeping through the edges of my mind. Another time, another dream and, sadly, another justification for not going home.

That time something terrible happened.

Back when I'd first come to Canada, I had brought with me the money that my cousin Ken had given me for my fifteenth birthday, plus interest. It helped pay for my journalism studies at Ryerson Polytechnic Institute.

I'd made two promises to Ken, and kept the first one: I got my degree, then a job as a television news reporter with the Canadian Broadcasting Corporation (CBC). I volunteered to work with children from poor families.

But the second promise, to write a book with him about our family history, took a back seat. Over the next few years, there was always a commitment, always an expense preventing me from returning to Jamaica to work with him on the book, although the promise sat there in the back of my mind.

Then, one day while I was preparing a story for the late-night TV news, the phone on my desk rang.

"Call your sister in Jamaica," Hamlin said. "Something about Ken."

I called Pat right away.

"He's sick," she told me. "All of a sudden, he can't even move his legs. The doctors say they've never seen anything like it."

The flight home used up all my small savings, but that didn't matter. Two days later I rushed in to the intensive care ward at the University Hospital in Kingston.

I tried to hug Ken, but he didn't hug back. He just lay there. He had lost the use of his arms as well as his legs.

"Scratch the top of my head for me ..." he asked weakly, his voice slurred. "Please ..."

I scratched his head and dampened his soft hair with huge, unstoppable tears.

Ken was the proudest, most fiercely independent person I had ever known. I knew he would sooner die than not be able to care for himself. These thoughts raced around and around in my mind as I held Ken's useless hands between mine.

I visited him for hours every day, sometimes alone, sometimes with my sister Pat. I sat there next to his bed talking, telling him about Canada and Toronto and my job and my husband and our two lovely daughters. His sisters and brother joined us at the bedside.

After a week, Ken miraculously started to improve. He was still in bed, of course, but now could actually sit up by himself. His colour came back and his voice was clearer, stronger, much more like his old voice.

He was so much better and there were so many relatives around that I felt sure he wouldn't miss me if I went back to Toronto. I said goodbye and kissed him.

This time, he asked for two promises.

"Come back home so we can write the book together," he said. "And make sure you get the four-poster bed from Granny's house before someone uses it for firewood." We laughed companionably as he reminded me of the bed left to him by my great-grandmother. He had decreed that the bed should be mine.

I promised. "I'll be back in six months," I said.

He smiled and said, "It's OK. I'm not going anywhere."

I loved this man, deeply. As I held on to his hand, holding back the tears, I realized that I was the closest thing to a daughter that Ken had ever known. I didn't know how I was going to keep these two promises, but I was determined that I would.

One Sunday morning in the spring, just four months later, the phone rang. It was Ken's sister Glenor. She, my sister Pat, and I had sat beside Ken's hospital bed in Jamaica.

"Hya?" she said softly, in her unmistakable Jamaican lilt, calling me by my childhood pet name.

"Don't say anything, Glenor," I whispered. "I don't want to hear."

"I'm really sorry."

"I promised to go back, Glenor. I thought I had time."

I was babbling, too shocked to console Glenor, who had lost a beloved brother.

On the four-hour flight to Kingston I had a lot of time for memories. Sweet memories of Ken. His generosity, his intelligence, his beauty. But all the while during those four endless hours, something nagged at me.

I'd had a dream, just a few days earlier.

In the dream, I picked green fruit from my mother's

orange tree and dug up yams from her garden. Jamaicans will tell you that a dream like that warns of double sadness: disappointment and death.

My sophisticated Canadian self told me to ignore it. So I did just that and continued with my life. And days later, there I was, on a plane to Jamaica, to attend Ken's funeral.

~

Now, years later, came the dream about losing my teeth. Every logical bone in my body said there was no valid reason to go home. But like the atheist who half believes in God in the wee, dark hours of the night, I couldn't shake the dream. What if it was a warning from above?

"You're a hopeless idiot," I told myself. "You don't really believe in dreams."

Still, I took some overdue vacation time, booked a flight, and started packing.

I had made precious few trips to Jamaica in the past fifteen years. It was wonderful to be home. But I spent most of my time covertly checking loved ones for intimations of mortality.

My mother was a little shorter, a little older, her hair a little more grey. But her smooth, light-brown skin was radiant, and she was obviously strong and healthy. As always, she enveloped me with hugs, love, and inspiration.

My father looked exactly the way I had left him. His handsome face glowed with good health.

But the dream was still in my head. Urgently, I ran through the list of every relative and friend whom I loved.

"How is Aunt Birdie? And Uncle Son? And the children? How is ..."

My mother cut off my anxious babble with, "Everybody's healthy and well. Stop worrying and come have some soup!"

Chapter Nineteen

The Painting

Mine was already the immigrant success story. I had thrown myself into my new life in Canada and was grateful for it all: my husband and children, my job and home, my relatives, friends, and neighbours.

Sometimes, success can make you feel that you have no right to yearn for anything else. But I had a secret: sometimes I missed my Jamaican family and home so badly, it felt like a physical ache.

I missed the things that I had grown up with, taken for granted, and never imagined I would ever yearn for: the easy familiarity of almost every person who passed by our gate; the smell of the trees and flowers; the sounds of village life. I even missed the over-eager rooster crowing his head off at four a.m., triggering, across the valley, a chorus of dogs barking, cows mooing, donkeys braying, and goats bleating.

Years before, I received a postcard from Jamaica, sent by a long-time friend. Gazing at the image on the card, I felt as though I had landed plunk in the middle of the scene. I could almost feel the Jamaican sunshine on my face.

Rich layers of detail revealed the vibrant life of a

village in the Jamaican countryside. In the centre, a pastel-coloured, octagonal-shaped house with mullioned windows and small front verandah stood small and proud; in the side yard, a large bunch of bananas, turning yellow, was ready to be picked from its tree; a dog ran behind a bicycle; children, on their way to school, were dressed in sharply ironed blue tunics and short-sleeved white shirts but looked ready to break into play at any moment.

My pulse raced at the familiar sight. This is where I come from, I thought, feeling a pang of homesickness. I knew this place like the back of my hand. It was a world in which virtually no one passed another without a greeting. And when someone asked, "How are you?" they not only meant it – they expected a full report.

It was a place where some people were lucky enough to get jobs at the bauxite mines, or as a teacher, gardener, or housekeeper, but most made a living from farming. The farms were generally small, as were the profits they yielded. Those small profits, in turn, were spent on the basics of life: food, clothing, shelter; school books and uniforms for the children; a family Bible; and a modest offering in the collection plate at church on Sunday morning.

Throughout the university years, then the early years of launching my career and starting a family of my own, I yearned to buy a painting that reminded me of home. But I saw art as something for the future, once the necessities of life had been accounted for.

But when that postcard arrived from Jamaica, I made a pledge: "One day when I have money, I am going to track down this artist and commission her to make me a painting of Jamaican country life!"

I tucked the card away for safekeeping and started saving dollar bills. Once a year or so, I took the card out of my dresser drawer and looked at it, then put it back, right under my small wooden box with its growing pile of money.

Not long after, on a stroll through a Birks store in downtown Toronto, a sculpture of a waterfowl caught my eye. It was a mallard, beautifully carved and painted in rich jewel-tones. Although – living in the city – I had never seen a live mallard, I had seen enough photographs of them to know that this waterfowl was an icon of Canadian country life, something I planned to experience some day.

Sorely tempted, I nearly bought the carving, reasoning that it was far more affordable than a painting. But it was not a priority, I told myself, and put the sculpture back on the display table.

And it wasn't *the* painting.

~

My trip home, courtesy of the dream about losing my teeth, was full of love and hugs and food and family stories.

On my last full day on the island, I toured the art gallery whose name and address were printed on the back of that postcard: Harmony Hall, a former Methodist manse located near Ocho Rios in the parish of St. Ann. Although I wasn't ready yet to commission *the* painting, I wanted the artist's address so that when the time came – as I knew it surely would – I would know where to find her.

"Eve Foster?" the gallery worker asked. "We don't carry her work anymore. I don't think she's even painting these days."

My heart sank. I asked whether anyone there knew how I could find Eve. "I would like her to know how much joy I got from that simple postcard of her painting," I said.

But no one seemed to know her address.

That night, a woman phoned.

"My name is Annabella," she said. "Eve Foster is my friend. I hear you want to write to her. I have her address. She lives in a village in Devon, England. Have you paper and pen?"

It was all said in one stream of words. I grabbed paper and pen and wrote it all down. Then, after receiving my surprised thanks, Annabella said a quick goodbye and was gone.

I wrote the letter to Eve on the flight back to Canada and posted it shortly after my arrival.

Her reply came a few weeks later. In the first paragraphs, she wrote of her love for the Jamaican countryside she had left behind. She said my letter had touched her, in part because I described some of what she felt whenever she created one of her Jamaican paintings: a yearning for her childhood home.

Her next words were therefore shocking.

"I am going blind," she wrote.

How absolutely awful, I thought. For someone to have such an eye for detail – to be so talented an artist – and to lose her sight.

I swallowed hard and continued to read.

"I have a few good days. They don't come around very often now, but when they do, I could have a try at making you a painting."

How courageous, I thought. But a bit unrealistic, perhaps? I read on.

"At this rate, it could take me years to complete it. And even then, it may not be good enough. Can you be patient? If you can, then I will surely try. If you don't like the painting when completed, you are not obligated to buy it."

She had thrown me a curve ball, all right. Was it wise, I wondered, to pursue this? After all, I wasn't ready for the painting just then – I was still saving dollar bills in my wooden box. Further, this would be the first original painting I would buy. And I knew that Jamaica had produced many gifted painters, most quite capable of painting scenes of country life. Did I trust Eve, failing eyesight and all, to make me a painting?

During a brief discussion with my husband, I realized that I had already decided.

"If you will make me a painting," I wrote back to Eve, "then I will accept it and pay you for it. Do not worry about the number of years it takes. I will use that time to save up for it. And Eve: THANK YOU."

~

Over the next several months, our family life continued as it had before: two children in school; a happy marriage; two busy careers; community service; time spent with family; lots of school homework and lots of housework; paying the mortgage every month end.

Hamlin and I had also become loving caretakers of a farm owned by his relatives in Warkworth, an hour and a half east of Toronto. We grabbed the opportunity, grateful that our children would have the chance to experience country life.

Every Friday evening, we packed children, pet dog, toys, food, and ourselves into the car, drove the ninety minutes, unpacked in a hurry, stoked up the old wood stove, and shivered under blankets while the farmhouse warmed up. And then our weekend life would begin.

In our previous visits to the village, we had never encountered another black family. But we had been warned that some country folk did not take kindly to weekenders, and we shouldn't take it personally.

"This is the kind of village," said one long-time weekender, "where it takes twelve years before they invite you to join the hockey team, but twenty years before they pass you the puck!"

I gave a silent prayer of thanks that my family didn't play hockey and decided to keep an open mind.

We took to the countryside like ducks to water. The children marvelled at the star-filled night sky, the trees that seemed to be everywhere, the streams and ponds on the many properties we passed. The long country roads, dotted by old Ontario farmhouses built of red brick or white board and batten trimmed with green shutters and doors.

The four of us were always delighted by the bounty of vegetables and fruit left for sale on stands by the road-side in front of farmers' houses. Even more intriguing was the honour system that the absent farmers used to conduct business while they tended their fields or live-stock or took a trip into town, leaving their market stands unsupervised.

A simple sign, usually handwritten on brown card-board, told you the price of things. You picked up the quantity of tomatoes or beets or cucumbers or corn that you wanted and dropped your payment through a slit in the plastic lid of a coffee can. It was as if it had never occurred to either the farmers or their customers that someone could simply pick up the can of money – and the produce – and walk away.

I also appreciated the down-to-earth ways of our neighbours and the expressions they used. After all, I, too, came from a place where people often spoke in prov-erbs and metaphors.

"That guy was three sheets to the wind," I overheard a woman say, describing someone who'd gotten himself totally drunk at a local event.

"I tell you, she was only half a sandwich short of a picnic," said our friend Joyce about a woman she claimed was crazy. Joyce owned an antique store on the main street in the village.

"It was an all-out donnybrook," said Ron, our neighbour from two farms over, as he reported to us on a fist fight that turned into a brawl at a recent dance.

And then, when you least expected it, along came a touch of true elegance. The Pork Producers' Ball turned out to be the same thing our friends John and Jayne had mentioned when they called to invite us to "the pig farmers' dance," and it was indeed elegant. The beautiful lady in fancy dress who waved us over with a brilliant smile was none other than Jayne. John, whom I'd only ever seen wearing rugged coveralls while driving his tractor or mucking out the strong-smelling pig barn, walked up to us wearing a well-cut suit and minutes later waltzed me across the floor in a movement as light as a feather in a gentle breeze.

During the summer holidays, our children took care of one of the neighbours' pigs, and later adopted three goslings who quickly became full-grown geese with personalities of their own. Hamlin named them Huey, Dewey, and Louie, and we all swore that they smiled whenever Nikisha and Lauren showed up with their buckets of grain to feed them.

Weekends and holidays in the country, weekdays in the city: it was a harmonious balance between town and country, and we were grateful for it.

～

On a weekday evening in the fall, the telephone rang. On the other end, it seemed, was Elizabeth, Queen of Britain.

"Is this Cynthia Reyes?" she inquired in a posh voice.

"It is, indeed!" I replied, summoning my best voice.

"My name is Anna Gosset," said the somewhat stern voice. "I am the sister-in-law of Eve Foster."

She pronounced Eve's last name in the accent of the English upper class, making it sound like "Fosstah."

"Eve has sent something for you and I have it here. There is only one problem. You are in Toronto and I am at least two hours away."

"Where do you live?" I asked.

"Warkworth," she replied, pronouncing it "Walkwuth."

"I know Warkworth very well," I said. "We live there on weekends."

She didn't miss a beat. "I don't think you heard me correctly," she countered. "I said I live in Warkworth."

"And so do I."

Into the silence, I described the exact location of Warkworth, a village northeast of Toronto.

"Your husband's relatives have a farm there? And where is this farm?"

Now I was feeling as though I had been called to the headmistress's office to explain my role in some misdemeanour.

As I described the location of the farm – patiently, slowly, trying to keep the edge out of my voice – her silence was so profound that I had to ask, "Are you still there?"

"My dear," she said slowly, "I know your farmhouse very well. For years I would go there every week, sometimes several times a week. The woman who lived there was an artist."

It was my turn to be taken aback. "Yes, she was an artist. But why did you visit the house so many times?"

"My husband carved sculptures of Canadian waterfowl. And that artist painted on the colours. I must have visited your house a hundred times."

Somewhere, there is a goose walking over my grave, I thought, as an eerie feeling moved from the top of my head down to my toes.

My caller proceeded to describe the farmhouse in detail: the huge weeping willow tree at the front of the property; the long driveway leading up to the house; the sloping old grey barn to the right of the driveway; the primitive mudroom, once the tiny family home, now a storage room cum side entrance to the house; the massive great room that housed an open kitchen and dining room, its ceiling covered entirely with burnished planks of maple wood; the large family room with its many floor-to-ceiling bookshelves; the splendidly wide and solid maple staircase going up to the second floor. It was an honest to goodness, well-built, solid Ontario farmhouse, dating back to the late 1800s.

"I think I have to take a seat," I told Anna, my voice shaking now.

"I think I will, too," she replied, sounding almost vulnerable.

And then another surprise was revealed. As Anna talked, it dawned on me that her husband was the well-known Canadian waterfowl sculptor Christopher Gosset. It was his beautifully carved mallard that I had nearly bought in the Birks store in Toronto years earlier.

Then I realized that Anna had not provided any information about the item that Eve had asked her to deliver to me.

"May I ask what is the item that Eve sent?"

"She sent you a painting. It appears that she worked feverishly at it whenever the light and her eyesight were good. She was determined to do it for you while she still could."

~

Two days later, we showed up at Anna and Christopher's farm. There was a long moment before anyone spoke, and then everyone spoke at once.

Christopher brought out a large rectangular case, which contained Eve's painting. At the same time, Anna handed me a letter from Eve. Nervously, I read it aloud to Hamlin.

"Dear Cynthia, I had to make this painting while I had some sight left. I hope you will like it. Please do not be afraid to let me know if you don't. If you decide to keep it, please pay me when you can afford to. I know you were expecting to wait a few years, so please do not feel pressured, especially with Christmas so close. You can pay me in partial amounts, and do so when you can."

The painting was – as I had hoped – a vivid portrait of life in a Jamaican village. It bustled with the telling details of country life.

Children play on the roadside on their way to school. A dilapidated minibus is filled to overflowing with passengers and their belongings. A goat ambles along the top of a stone wall. In the doorway of the small church to the right where the road curves, barely perceptible is the pastor in his clerical collar, talking to a woman who is dressed to the nines even though it is a weekday. And taking pride of place in the centre of the scene, a charming little yellow wooden house, surrounded by fruit trees and a variety of brilliant Jamaican shrubs and flowers.

In the foreground, across from the small house, is a fenced field, and in it are cattle, branded with the initials "BG" – a sign that they belong to the Gosset farm, Eve and Christopher's beloved family homestead in Hanover, Jamaica. In the distance, the peaceful countryside: trees, shrubs, and far-off mountains; fluffy white clouds floating under a blue sky, birds swooping below them; the hint of other villages beyond.

Life in the Jamaican countryside as remembered by a woman in the English countryside and captured on canvas for a younger woman in Canada whom she had never met.

Years later, as the snow piled up outside our Canadian house, when the skies turned grey and I felt a million miles away from the countryside of my childhood, I was warmed by the sun of that painting, by the unchanged scenery, and by memories of the trust and perseverance that spanned thousands of miles to produce it.

Chapter Twenty

Paradise Regained

What was behind the tall fence and thick evergreens that created such a forbidding barrier between this place and the outside world? I peered between the bars of the black wrought-iron gate, trying to find out.

Slowly, I discerned the unmistakable gurgle and splash of water flowing over stones. It was the sound of magic; the sound of childhood.

A For Sale sign beckoned in front of the property, and in that moment, a new possibility opened.

The old farm in Warkworth was now someone else's home, no longer our weekend and summer retreat. The children had given up Huey, Dewey, and Louie to our friend Allison, who had kindly agreed to adopt them.

All four of us had fallen hard for country life. We missed the farm, the people, the rolling landscape, the star-filled black velvet sky. We often talked about buying a place of our own in the country "one of these days."

Days after seeing the For Sale sign on this property, an hour east of Toronto, and listening to the sound of falling water, Hamlin and I walked through the open gates, through the barricade of evergreens, alongside a small white house, and stopped at a sight that literally took our breath away.

A large emerald-green lawn sprawled in front of the house. To its left was a big pond. In the centre of the pond, covered with light pink roses, was a small island. Hydrangea shrubs bearing large white flowers circled two-thirds of the pond's edge. Behind them was an imposing backdrop of tall evergreen cedars that formed a dense, dark-green curtain.

The call of a cardinal pierced the silence; a dragonfly touched down on the water, creating small ripples on the placid surface of the pond.

The source of the falling water was to the right, a small stream that splashed its way downhill over a series of rocks and levels, with small yellow flowers clinging to its banks. A long, narrow wooden bridge, its handrails silver-grey with age, spanned the stream where it widened before merging with the pond.

Birds swooped into the pond and swooped back out, while others sang to each other hidden on their perches on the branches of tall trees. Across the bridge and up another slope was a long bench under a huge tree that soared into the sky.

A tree to climb, came the thought.

A small, lonely blue-green shed stood to the left. Masses of daylilies almost surrounded it. Beyond the shed was the beginning of a forest glade, a tantalizing hint of more to come.

It was all achingly, piercingly familiar. I held my breath, fearful that even breathing would cause it all to vanish.

"Home," said my heart.

Slowly I turned to look at the house. A small thing, an old thing, its walls stuccoed a white so tired it looked almost pink. Its roof and shutters were forest green, with tall French doors and windows trimmed in the same shade. A verandah stretched across the front of the house. Beyond it, in the centre of a sunroom, I could see a dining table and chairs that seemed to be waiting for us to come in and have a meal.

I realized that I was holding my breath and exhaled deeply, shaking my head to see if the house was an illusion. But it was no illusion. I would have recognized this place even if it had been on the moon. This was the northern version of my childhood home in the Caribbean. It was the place my family had left behind when I was only six years old, the place that I had carried in my heart ever since. This was my Narnia.

I clutched Hamlin's hand and said, "This place feels like home."

He squeezed my hand, drew me close, and whispered, "I know."

Decades and three thousand miles away, my childhood paradise was manifesting itself before me: acres of fields, trees, and water galore; a small house (more cottage than house) with green trim and a verandah.

Along with a yearning to recapture part of my childhood came a powerful urge to own a little piece of Canadian history, something in which I, the immigrant, had no ancestry, only an avid interest. The combination was irresistible.

When we showed it to our children, now ages six and thirteen, and they fell instantly in love with it, their eyes shining, our desire to own it became even stronger.

A mysterious force had taken possession of our minds. To counteract it, Hamlin and I decided to be cautious.

"Saner heads must prevail," we told ourselves, over and over. It was the early nineties, and inflation had taken a bite out of our earnings. This was not the time for profligate spending.

So we tallied up and compared the lists of pros and cons. The sale of our house in Toronto would help, but we knew we would have to rent a place in Toronto for times when work kept us in the city.

Months passed. We checked everything twice, and made our offer to purchase. All of the contents we were buying along with the house were clearly identified in the offer. The only things we didn't itemize were the names and titles of the hundreds of old books on the living-room shelves.

"These books came with the house," said the owner as I crouched down in front of a bookcase, pen and notebook at the ready. "They have been here for decades. No need to bother writing down each title. I would never dream of removing them."

I closed my notebook, put my pen away, and went outside to drink in the air by the pond. The coming Christmas, I thought, would be the most special in years. I could see our family skating on the pond and drinking hot cider or hot chocolate by the massive fireplace in the living room, each of us curled up with a good book.

Chapter Twenty-one

Betrayal and Loss

Though it was not that far from Toronto, our new house in the country was a secret place, hidden from the outside world.

Tall, thick evergreen hedges encircled the property; few people, except for some elderly neighbours, knew what was on the other side. The house was originally built as a fishing lodge in the late 1800s by a prominent Canadian family, and, according to local legend, a former prime minister had spent "drunken weekends" there. Over the decades, subsequent owners added a small room here and there, but had kept the additions as sympathetic to the original as possible.

The large living room and stone fireplace were original. The smoke of many wood fires had darkened the shade of the stone around the hearth. With sunlight streaming in over them, the maple floors gleamed with the precious patina that comes from over a hundred years of living and good care.

It was a wonderful place. A special place. And, incredibly, it was ours.

Moving day came. My husband, two daughters, pet dog, and I arrived at our new home, breathless with excitement. It was everything that we remembered, except that the skies seemed especially blue that day and the birdsong particularly pretty.

Before long, beds were made, personal items placed in each room, and a first meal cooked and eaten with pleasure. Then came a leisurely walk – the children gleefully running ahead, the dog barking in excitement – across the various bridges, through the glades and forest, and back to the house for a rest in the living room.

It was then that we made an astonishing discovery: all of the old hardcover books had been removed; in their place were paperbacks and an assortment of outdated school textbooks.

It made no sense. Our earlier walk-through had revealed that all of the furniture and household items we had bought from the previous owners were accounted for. But the books that were supposed to have been part of the deal were missing.

I beat back a pang of alarm by telling myself that someone had simply made a mistake. Surely the books would be returned.

"I would never dream of removing them," the former owner had insisted.

Gone were the wonderful old books by authors whose writing I loved: C.S. Lewis, whose Narnia chronicles had seemed particularly at home in this house; William Shakespeare; Catherine Parr Traill and Susanna Moodie; Jane Austen; Somerset Maugham; Charles Dickens; Mark Twain; poets Emily Dickinson, Virgil, Tennyson, T.S. Eliot, and many more. Gone was the musty old-book smell I had loved since childhood.

When we finally tracked him down, the former owner told us that he had discovered, just before moving, that the books were primarily first editions and very valuable. He had sold them all to an auctioneer.

"No," he said, "I don't remember telling you that those particular books were included in the purchase price of the house."

Nor, he said, did he remember telling us there was no need to record the name of each book on the list of items to be left behind. Then he said goodbye.

I could have kicked myself. A serious book lover knows that books can be more important than furniture. Why, then, had I not taken the time to itemize each of the hundreds of books on the shelves? How could I have been so stupid?

For months the bookcases seemed bereft, silently waiting for their precious contents to be returned. In the years to come, they gradually filled up with books we had loved, books we went out and bought, and books we were given. Lewis, Shakespeare, Twain, Austen, Auden, and Dickinson would rub shoulders with Rachel Manley, Margaret Laurence, Louise Bennett, Isabel Allende, Derek Walcott, and other writers from Canada, the Caribbean, and Latin America. But back then, my only consolation was a secret, angry hope that "time wounds all heels."

~

"Ah! There's nothing like staying home for real comfort," Jane Austen wrote. Indeed. The kitchen was small, the back bedroom cold, but the good times in this place were particularly good: fishing or canoeing on the two ponds in the summer, skating on the large pond in winter.

The ponds did not freeze that first Christmas but turned into thick ice by mid-winter. One Sunday we had a skating party. Friends and relatives of all ages glided around the ice. The sound of happy laughter pealed across the grounds as adults and children competed, collided, and sometimes went sprawling.

The weather on the first Easter weekend was perfect

for an Easter egg hunt. With so many places to hide the eggs on the seven acres surrounding the house, Hamlin and I forgot where most of them were. We enjoyed the hunt almost as much as the children, trying to keep up with them as they raced from glades to woods and across bridges.

Later, we discovered that our dog Barclay had quietly sniffed out some of the chocolate eggs himself.

"Ew, yuck!" the children yelled. "Barclay stinks!"

That night his obnoxious odour nearly suffocated us, and we ran out onto the grounds laughing. Even the stars in the dark velvet sky seemed to be twinkling with humour as Barclay pranced around us, unaware that his terrible smell was the source of our hilarity. We learned later that chocolate was bad for dogs, but Barclay emerged from his adventure without any sign of injury.

Every walk through the grounds evoked a sense of deep gratitude for our good fortune. One early spring, as we walked through a glade and approached the smaller pond, an orange blob (which we had taken for a plastic bag, trapped in the frozen water) suddenly started to move. We realized that we were witnessing the springtime awakening of a school of orange-coloured fish: these were the full-grown versions of the tiny goldfish the children and I had released into the pond just a few springs before.

Spring was always a time of wonder, and the large pond became our own private nature channel. Birds we had never seen or heard of stopped in for a visit, sending us scurrying for the binoculars and our book of birds.

We marvelled at the speed with which our resident kingfisher dove to snatch its prey from the water. We knew the pair of mallards would return to the pond each spring, but we never knew when, or how many ducklings they would hatch, or when the parents would start teaching their offspring to swim and dive.

One year, the family was joined by a Canada goose, which settled in as though it had been part of the duck family all along. The children and I thought this a heartwarming sight, but Hamlin was afraid the pond would soon be taken over by its brethren and decided to take action. He had read somewhere that the only way to get rid of geese was to pretend to be a swan because the two birds do not happily coexist.

He grabbed two large white towels and ran around the pond flapping his arms like large wings. The girls and I clutched our stomachs and laughed till we fell to the ground. His technique seemed to work, however. The goose left.

One Saturday, in the middle of a steady spring rain, eight wood ducks landed on the pond and stayed for hours, leaving us all to wonder what kind of mischievous mood had struck the Creator when he or she decided to paint brilliantly coloured geometric shapes on the birds' feathery coats and outline each shape in white.

One fall day, an unexpected snowfall began, with the largest and fluffiest snowflakes we had ever seen. The four of us ran outside, hands outstretched to catch the flakes, our dog barking happily around us. It seemed we had entered a very large snow globe.

The girls each claimed a favourite place on the grounds.

Nikisha loved the glades, where she strolled, fed the fish, and paddled in her canoe in the big pond.

Lauren had a "secret hiding place," as she called it: a cool and private spot beneath the lacy branches of an evergreen that completely sheltered a small section of the stream and banks as the water flowed silently through. The rest of us always felt privileged when invited to join her there. We talked about our favourite things and made up stories together.

"May the countryside and gliding valley streams

content me," wrote the poet Virgil. For Hamlin, this place meant two things: peace, and family. I could see the cares fall away from his shoulders and contentment cover him like a blanket whenever we arrived here from our jobs in the city.

~

Living here, I understood for the first time how author Samuel Clemens (known as Mark Twain) could have so loved his home in Hartford, Connecticut, which he believed had both a heart and a soul. "We never came home from an absence that its face did not light up and speak out in eloquent welcome – and we could not enter it unmoved."

Unforeseen circumstances later forced Clemens, his wife, Olivia, and their family to move from their home and later sell it. We never thought the same would happen to us. We imagined passing it down, over the decades, from generation to generation.

Then, after a few years in this house, we came up against two immovable objects: the brutal economic recession of the mid nineties, and my parents' ill health. My father's illness was critical: cancer. My parents needed our help. We were glad we had rented a Toronto house. It was conveniently situated close to the hospitals and clinics where my parents had their medical appointments. But it was yet another expense. We juggled and re-juggled our finances over the next few years till there were too many balls to catch. It was time to make a sacrifice.

Sometimes, things seem to come full circle. For the first time, I sat my family down and told them about the loss of my first childhood home, followed by the huge sacrifice my parents had made to provide us with a proper house to live in. I explained how, during the lengthy separation after my father left for England, he and my mother never saw each other, never even spoke to each other.

Nikisha and Lauren had tears in their eyes. But they were facing their own loss. The knowledge of their grandparents' earlier sacrifices didn't change that fact. Nor did it eliminate the pain that Hamlin and I felt. Our children were losing their own Narnia, my husband his peaceful place, and I my childhood home for the second time.

The poet Wordsworth was right: the special places of childhood cannot be frozen in time for our own enjoyment. Although I had regained "the hour of splendour in the grass, of glory in the flower," our family would "find strength" and move on.

Home would just have to be somewhere else.

Chapter Twenty-two

A Secret Garden

In the months while we waited for the sale of our small Ontario cottage and enchanting grounds to be completed, my thoughts swung between that loss and an even bigger one, one that drew closer and closer.

My father's cancer was pronounced incurable. Doctor after doctor had examined him, even operated on him, and finally given us the news no family wants to hear. All that was left now was for him to be made comfortable in his final months in the Jamaican mountainside home he and my mother had both worked so hard to build.

Though my mother always said she was managing "just fine" back in the family home, I didn't entirely believe her. I constantly wished I could be there to help. But work and other obligations – such as finding a new home – kept me in Canada in those months.

My parents now had a phone in their home, so I settled for calling them often, helping them financially, and praying for them every day. I prayed that my father would be spared the pain that often comes with the end-stage of cancer; that my mother would find strength, comfort, and someone reliable to help them in this time.

~

On the way home from shopping one Saturday, I glimpsed an exquisite patch of purple irises blooming under a front window of an old stone house.

We hadn't even purchased a new house yet, but I knew that when we did, I would want to have a garden with flowers – flowers such as these luminous, deep-purple irises.

I asked Hamlin to stop the car so I could approach the woman who was tending to them. Trowel in hand, she straightened up and returned my greeting as though she was used to strangers interrupting her gardening.

"I like the colour of your purple irises," I said. "I see that they've outgrown their spot. So I wonder if, when you're dividing them, I could buy some from you. I'll have my own garden then, and would be happy to pay you a good price."

Most gardeners like their plants to be admired, and so did this one. Her smile lit up her face, but she refused to sell her flowers to me, saying she would be happy to give some to me instead.

A sensible person would have gladly accepted. Not I.

"I simply can't do that," I found myself replying. 'It wouldn't be right. We don't even know each other."

Later I realized how false this might have sounded. After all, I had walked straight into her garden and boldly told her it was time to divide her iris patch and sell some of the flowers to me.

The woman said, gently, "Would you like to see the rest of the garden?"

"That would be wonderful!" I replied. I motioned for Hamlin to join us.

"I'm Marion," she said.

Hamlin and I introduced ourselves and happily trailed

behind her down the garden path. As we turned the corner around a small stone cottage next to the main house, we were hit with a powerful fragrance, then beheld what I can only describe as a series of secret gardens.

Hidden behind the small stone cottage were the ruins of a set of former stables. Only the half-walls of each stable remained, providing a partition from one small garden to the next. Climbing hydrangea, purple panicles of wisteria, and fragrant yellow sweet alyssum tumbled and sprawled along the back wall of the stables.

In one stall was the biggest tree peony I had ever seen, bearing large, delicate pink flowers. On the ground around it lay low-growing light blue forget-me-nots and a variety of springtime perennials, some blooming, some in bud. Hosta of different hues and leaf shapes seemed to be everywhere. Bleeding heart peonies were in full bloom.

In another stall was a small fishpond, surrounded by yet more flowers. In yet another, a green and gold garden plaque declaring that "One is closer to God's heart in the garden than anywhere else on earth" floated above a floor of green ground cover.

Astonished at the beauty surrounding me, I hardly knew what to say. But what our host said next shocked me.

"We were away visiting our daughter for a month," she revealed, "and now the garden is so overgrown that, for the first time, we have been giving serious thought to selling the house."

She paused, a look of sorrow spreading across her face. "We love it dearly. But we're getting old, and it's probably foolish to keep it."

Remembering my own recent sacrifice, I said, "Oh, but you can't do that! It's obvious how much you love it."

At one a.m. the next morning, an idea jolted me awake,

and I got up and wrote a proposition to the owners of the secret garden.

"Since you are too stubborn to sell me the irises and I am too stubborn to accept them free of charge, I hereby offer to garden for you this spring and summer. If you agree, you will pay me in flowers. We can start with the purple irises!"

Hamlin read the letter during breakfast.

"You're a crazy woman," he said, laughing. "All that gardening – for a patch of iris."

But we both knew that this was not really about a patch of iris. We both knew that, at this time in our lives, helping an elderly couple get through a challenging time in their lives was a good thing. An elderly couple, roughly the same age as my parents.

Thus did I become a volunteer gardener for Marion and her husband, Henry.

Twice a week, from spring to fall, I appeared in their garden, early in the morning or in the evening, sometimes knocking at their door to say a quick hello, most times carrying out my chores unannounced and quietly leaving. I knew where everything was kept – the clippers, the spade and hoe, the garden fork, trowels, the hose, and the watering can – which made for an easy routine.

It was hard work, I realize now. But back then, in the most beautiful garden I had ever known, it hardly felt like work. I felt sheltered, healed, at peace. This was my own secret garden. The place where I confided to the earth, the air, the birds, and the plants what was going on inside my heart.

Often silently and sometimes aloud, I confided my hopes that my parents and family would find strength in this time, and that Hamlin, our daughters, and I would find happiness in our next home.

Chapter Twenty-three

"Solid and Sensible"

Harry the real estate agent had been a constant in our lives, a kind of uncle figure to Hamlin and me. He loved our children. And his advice went far beyond that of a real estate agent.

It seemed that, having set us on the right path, he didn't want to venture too far from us, in case we were tempted to screw up again. Or so Hamlin and I joked from time to time. Fact is, we were very grateful for Harry.

Recently, he had helped us negotiate the sale of our beloved cottage, helped to console me when my father's illness took a turn for the worse, and phoned repeatedly to reassure us that we'd get through this awful stage in our lives. Things would get better.

The first order of business was to find a new place to live.

"We'll find you a good home," Harry said.

Harry was over eighty years old now, but still had his real estate business and a partner to help him. We knew, though, that finding our family a new home was something he wouldn't entrust to anyone but himself.

He knew what we were looking for and was determined to find it.

"We don't care about history," I told him, tearing up at memories of the magical place we had just agreed to sell to another family.

"And it doesn't have to be charming," said Hamlin. "It has to be warm, bright, have a few acres, and be a solid, sensible house not too far from Toronto. That's what matters."

Harry smiled.

"They've really grown up," I imagined him thinking. "Charm was all they talked about when I was searching for their first home. Now it doesn't even make the list."

But Harry just nodded in agreement. He was still a man of few words.

Harry searched and searched, while we waited and waited, knowing we were in excellent hands. He took us to see a few houses and properties, walked the grounds with us, inspected the houses with us, muttering a comment or two about the negatives, pointing out a few things that were strong positives. But he wasn't satisfied. He kept searching.

Finally, one day, he called.

"I have a house I think you should see," he said.

Harry usually held his cards close to his chest, but his tone told us we had to drop everything and go right away. Lauren was home that afternoon and was eager to accompany us. Off we went.

Arriving at the end of a country road near the village of Brooklin, northeast of Toronto, we turned onto a gravel driveway and saw the house.

It was ... unusual. It was blue. It had a flat roof. It was L-shaped. It was not historic. And it was not charming. In fact, with the boxy shape and flat roof, it was entirely too modern looking, even a bit strange, for my taste.

"I don't like it," I told Hamlin and Lauren. "I can't see us living here."

"We have to see it," Hamlin replied. "Harry said the house was built to overlook the woods and the stream, so what we're looking at is actually the side of the house. Harry wouldn't steer us wrong."

Harry was waiting for us, looking slightly anxious but smiling.

We walked into a warm and sunny side entrance and into a bright, well-designed kitchen that overlooked the woods through enormous windows. To the right was a family room with cathedral ceilings, a stone fireplace, and still more large windows. There were no curtains in sight, but the house was in such a private spot that it didn't need them.

Lauren and I left the kitchen and walked through the other rooms, unconcerned by the fact that most were quite small, delighted by the "homeyness" of it and how the light poured in through every window.

"Hamlin!" I hollered down the hallway. "Come see the bedrooms!"

But Hamlin, the family's gourmet chef, was still admiring the kitchen.

"Dad's already thinking about all the meals he's going to cook in this kitchen," Lauren said, with a knowing smile.

Harry, meanwhile, was checking out the mechanics and calling to Hamlin to come and see.

Lauren and I went off to check out the grounds. We inspected the patches of woodlands, the small stream that ran by the side of the house, and the large one down below.

Years later, our family would discover that this was one of those unusual houses inspired by Frank Lloyd Wright's Usonian Model – the building the famous American architect had designed to house ordinary American families back in 1936. In Wright's approach,

homes were designed to sit well with nature, not domi-
nate it. His homes were often built into the side of their
wooded lots, with flat roofs, deep roof overhangs instead
of porches, and large windows to let the light in. And, in
the "public spaces" of the houses, the rooms led into one
another.

But we didn't know any of that at the time. What we
gradually realized that afternoon was that, thanks once
again to Harry, our family had found a new home.

There were no gardens, but that didn't worry us.

One late summer day, Henry and Marion showed up
at our new home with boxes and bags of plants. It was
the perfect gift for a place with an abundance of trees and
lawns but absolutely no flowers.

The biggest box contained what had started it all: a
patch of purple iris, now being delivered to us by a couple
we had grown to care for. Hamlin and I waved a fond
goodbye to them as they drove away, looked at each other,
and made a whoop of joy. Then we gave thanks for these
plants and for the grace of unexpected friendship.

Chapter Twenty-four

More Important Than Things

"Resentment is like a glass of poison a person drinks; then he sits down and waits for his enemy to die," said Nelson Mandela when asked to explain why he was not resentful over his imprisonment.

I marvelled at that statement, for I still had not forgiven the man who took the books from our beloved old cottage – and that was a small thing, by comparison.

Then, just months after we moved into our new house, he called us.

"I'm having heart surgery in just a few days," he said. "It's a risky operation, and I may not make it out alive."

'I'm sorry to hear this, and we wish you well," I replied.

"There's a reason why I'm calling," he continued. "I would like you to visit. Please ... Could you come? And would you also bring some large boxes? Several, if you have them."

It was not the first time we had spoken to him. Three years earlier – after the removal of the books but before we sold the place – we had called him with a question about the house and learned that, in the midst of an ice storm, he and his wife had fallen ill; their only relatives lived hundreds of miles away, and there was no one nearby whom they could call for help.

We had to make a decision: Would we help them or turn away? As we braved the icy driving conditions, we both admitted that, although we were going to their aid, the loss of the books still rankled.

Arriving at their house with boxes of groceries and other supplies, we found husband and wife weakened and in bed with a prolonged flu but adamantly refusing to go to the hospital. We cleaned the house, cooked enough food to last them for several days, did our best to make them comfortable, then checked in with them every day till they got better. Our unexpected help moved them to tears.

Now, a few years later, here we were, on our way to their home again, once again with mixed feelings.

"Are we complete idiots for even going there?" I asked Hamlin.

"Maybe not complete," he said with a laughed, "but close."

Husband and wife greeted us and led us through the large open spaces of their airy lakeside home. In the last room, large floor-to-ceiling shelves were packed tight with hardcover books, some leather-bound.

"These are the books I had promised you," said our host. "These are the books I should have left in the house when you bought it. I did sell the most valuable ones to an auctioneer, but I kept the rest."

He paused, then said, "I am so sorry. You deserved better. I hope you have brought many boxes. The books are all yours if you want them."

I walked slowly to a bookshelf and drew out first one book, then the next, till I had tenderly looked through at least a dozen. Some were novels – great English, American, and Canadian literature – while others were weighty non-fiction tomes about world history and war.

The names of the husband and wife who had owned the property several decades earlier were handwritten on the first page of every book, along with the name of the property and the date on which the book had been purchased or given. Several of the books were gifts from friends, and contained affectionate handwritten greetings below the names and dates.

My husband and I each selected only a few books from the shelves. Over the years we had bought so many to replace what he had taken away.

Our host, surprised, urged us to take them all.

"These can't be the only ones you brought," he said, staring at our two small boxes.

We sat with the couple for a while and exchanged memories of the main thing we had in common: a magical place that we had all loved and lost. The woman, who smiled often but said little, got up and left the room, but the man seemed reluctant to let us leave.

I suggested that he return the rest of the books to the old house. He seemed to consider it but did not reply.

"Why did you come?" he asked after a while.

"Because you asked us to. You seemed to really need us to come here."

"No," he said. "Why did you come and take care of my wife and me when we were alone and so ill? And why won't you take more of the books?"

"People," Hamlin said, softly and deliberately, "are more important than things."

Weeks after our visit, we heard that the man's surgery had been successful. But months later, he called to share sad news: his beloved wife, his longtime companion, was now in the advanced stages of Alzheimer's disease. She no longer recognized him.

"I would give anything I own – anything – to bring her back to her normal self," he said softly. He sounded as though he was crying.

It seemed that he finally understood the message my husband had intended. I know that I did.

Part Three

Visiting Home

Too rare, too rare,
grow now my visits here,
But once I knew each field,
each flower, each stick ...

~ Matthew Arnold

Chapter Twenty-five

Mama Throws Down the Gauntlet

J ust a few months after returning to the family home
in Jamaica, our beloved father died. He had been ill
with cancer and his death was expected. But no one is ever
really prepared for the death of a loved one.

All five children were living abroad: Yvonne and our
younger sister Jackie in Texas, while Pat, our younger
brother, Michael, and I lived in Canada. All of us went
home immediately.

We struggled with our own feelings of loss, but also
knew we had an immediate duty – to support our mother
through this time.

"No matter how tough it is for us," we said, "it's
tougher for Mama. It can't be easy to lose the love of
your life."

But Mama was focused on giving her beloved a good
funeral. It had rained the entire week, and on the day of
the funeral, everyone expected the flood rains to continue.

The wife of Mama's former pastor tried to console her.

"I am so sorry about all this rain," she said. "There's
going to be even more rain this afternoon."

"The rain will stop," Mama replied with quiet
conviction.

The pastor's wife pressed her point, trying to prepare Mama for the inevitable.

"What are you saying?" Mama shot back, raising her voice. "That our God won't stop the rain so my husband can have a fair afternoon for his funeral? Just think about all the people who have died – and some of them were awful people – but God still gave them a fair day for their funerals. You don't think my God will do the same for my husband, who was such a good man?"

The pastor's wife was speechless at this, and so were those of us who heard the conversation. Our mother's faith had proven true before, but this time it seemed that she had gone way out on a limb. All the weather experts were telling us to expect a flood, but she had thrown in her lot with the highest expert she knew.

There was to be no more discussion of the matter.

"Gee whiz," I whispered to my siblings. "Do you realize what just happened? Mama just told God that he'd better deliver – big time."

It's one thing to have faith, I thought, but quite another to put God on the spot. All our lives, we had heard our mother add a single caveat to her stated intentions: "DV." It was the acronym for *deo volente*, Latin for "God willing." But this time, no caveat.

Mama had thrown down the gauntlet.

It rained the rest of that morning. It rained in the early afternoon. It rained as we dressed, combed our hair, put on our shoes, and reached for our umbrellas. Then, as we headed for the front door, the rain stopped. It held off while our family drove to the church. It held off during the funeral service, as we sang the old familiar hymns, hugged our mother and one another, trying to stem the tears. The rain held off when the cemetery workers lowered our father's casket in the grave, while we thanked and bid farewell to family and friends and got into our cars.

Only as we drove down the steep hill from the church did the skies turn dark and the flood rains begin again.

Mama's children were left wondering if the time would ever come when our own faith would be that sure.

～

Although our father had been ill for a long time, his death was hard on our mother. She went through a year of mourning, a time in which her prayers grew more intense, her silences grew longer, and she seemed to occupy a separate space from the rest of us. She was still trying to say her goodbyes to Harold, and she needed to do it alone.

Earlier in their marriage, they had been apart for nearly ten years. When he finally came home from working in England, they still loved each other, but now they had to learn each other all over again: learn how to live together, how to talk and walk with each other, how to trust each other, how to show their love for each other.

As for the rest of us, ten years is a long time in the life of a child, and though we tried, none of us ever fully regained the closeness we had felt with our father. Our mother knew it. She had worried about it, and she had prayed about it.

I could only guess at how badly the two of them had suffered for that sacrifice, and as I matured, I had grown to love them fiercely and protectively because of it.

Months after our father's death, my mother came to visit us at our new home, the little blue house in the countryside. I had begged her to do this and she had. But now I saw her looking off into the distance, and heard her sigh, and I didn't know what to do.

Over and over again she'd shake her head, as though to clear it of regret. I didn't know what to say. She rarely shared her thoughts voluntarily, and I didn't know how to ask the questions that might have elicited the answers I sought.

She had loved us, fed us, challenged us, and encouraged us. She had tried to bolster our faith. And though my siblings and I tried our best to help her now, it seemed that only she could work her way back from wherever she was.

When she finally emerged from the dark woods of her grief, Mama's faith was, if anything, stronger, and her capacity for joy and laughter seemed even bigger.

Our beloved mother was back.

Chapter Twenty-six

A Lot of Grace

Mama now split her time between Canada and Jamaica – the warm months in Canada and the fall and winter in Jamaica. Three years after our father's death, I decided to visit her at the family home in Jamaica.

The flight to Kingston was full of people and luggage, as flights to Kingston often are.

Unlike the flights to Montego Bay, with tourists headed for all-inclusive resorts, flights to the capital city of Jamaica are usually crammed with Jamaicans returning home, accompanied by all the luggage the airline will allow.

I searched several overhead compartments and finally found a sliver of space and stuffed my carry-on luggage into it.

As I took my seat, I glanced to my right and did a double take. The young giant seated beside me looked very familiar. Staring openly for a moment, I finally figured it out. His sharp features and nut-brown skin reminded me of someone I knew: Roy, a cousin in my childhood village, who had left to join his parents in the United States when he was in his mid-teens. I had never seen him again, but had never forgotten his face and tall frame.

"Good morning," I said.

"Good morning," the young man replied. His accent was unmistakably Jamaican. His voice was surprisingly gentle, even shy.

"How are you?" he asked.

"How are you?" is not the same for people who grew up in a Jamaican village as it is in Toronto. It's a neighbourly question, requiring a real, even detailed answer. And now, sitting in an airplane full of Jamaicans, the question gave me pause. What to say to this well-mannered and familiar-looking young man, who was patiently waiting for an answer?

"As far as I know at this moment," I finally replied, rolling my eyes in self-mockery, "I am fine."

We both laughed.

Ahead of me were seven days with my beloved mother. I could barely contain my joy at the thought of being home with her again. I could almost hear the birds singing, the crickets chirping, and the goats bleating in the mountain air.

"What part of Jamaica are you from?" I asked my seatmate.

A smile instantly covered the young man's face as he named a village in a parish far away from my home village up in the mountains. I had never been there, but knew that it was in a country parish, like mine.

"Aha!" I replied. "I knew it! You're a country bumpkin, just like me."

Except, not just like me. I had left my whole family behind in Jamaica at the end of my teenage years, attended university in Toronto, been picked for a job with a prestigious Canadian organization, gotten married and raised a family, and won acclaim for my work.

This young man, on the other hand, looked like his adult life was barely beginning.

"What was life like in your village?" I asked.

His face lit up. Although his parents had gone abroad when he was very young, he said, he was raised by two loving people: his grandparents. They were poor, but his childhood was happy.

His was a story I knew well: Jamaican parents, trying to make a better life for themselves and their children, going abroad to where the jobs are.

In the fifties and early sixties, while Jamaica was still a colony of Britain, the jobs were mostly in England. In the four decades that followed, however, Jamaicans went in greater numbers to the US and Canada. Many of these men and women left their spouses behind with the children, but some travelled as couples to jobs abroad, leaving their children in the care of their own parents until they had established themselves in the new country.

As my seatmate spoke, I saw his grandmother taking him to school, his grandfather helping him with his homework. I saw them showing him how to shine his shoes, tuck his shirt into his trousers, buckle his belt, comb his hair, and go to church. I saw them reminding him to pray for his mother and father every night, to pray that God would keep them safe in Canada, one of the ways they tried to keep the boy's parents present in his young mind.

"As a teenager," my seatmate continued softly, "I was sent away from home to join my parents in Toronto." His friends envied him, he said, because everyone in his village wanted to come to Canada, the land of opportunity. He himself had been scared, about the new country, about the parents he no longer remembered. But his grandparents had been so hopeful for his life in Canada that he became hopeful, too.

I thought about his words "sent away from home." It must have been wrenching to leave his village. To leave the people he knew: the kids he'd gone to school with and played with, and the adults who had parented him, his grandparents.

Then, skipping over his time in Canada, he added, "Now I'm going home ... for good."

I had heard that phrase a hundred times, but it suddenly struck me as strange. Would anyone ever go home for bad?

Our breakfast arrived. About to start eating, I noticed a familiar ritual taking place beside me. Head bowed, lips moving in a whispered prayer, my seatmate was giving thanks for his meal. Not the quick for-what-we-are-about-to-receive-we-give-thee-thanks-oh-God, but a lengthy prayer.

Giving thanks to God for my meal had been a staple of my small-village upbringing in Jamaica. When had I stopped saying it? I couldn't recall.

My mother's face flashed into my mind. I knew she did, before every meal, exactly what this young man was doing. I felt a twinge of shame. Deciding to follow his example, I silently mumbled a prayer of my own. Unlike my seatmate, however, I chose the brief version and self-consciously raced through it.

For a while, we continued the flight in silence.

Then the young man asked me how long I had lived in Canada.

"Most of my life. How about you?"

He paused. "Not very long."

"How long?"

"Only about six years."

"So – are you finished with your studies? Or do you work?"

"I studied a bit."

"And then you worked?"

"Kinda."

A bleak look came over his face.

I took off my jacket and headed down the aisle to the washroom.

"Excuse me – but is this yours?" the young man asked me when I was back in my seat. He had something between his fingers and held it out toward me. It was a ring. I looked down at my hand, then back at the ring. It was a precious piece of jewelry, given to me years before by a beloved relative.

"Thank you so much," I said. "That is very kind of you."

Taking the ring, I slid it back on my finger, picturing how it had come loose. Before going to the washroom, I had tugged at my close-fitting jacket sleeve to remove the garment. The cloth had obviously become snagged on the protruding jewel and had pulled the ring off my finger. It had happened once before, and I had vowed to be more careful, but I had not been careful enough. How lucky I was to be sitting beside an honest person.

A few things became clear as we talked further. This young man had left home with great dreams but was now going home with troubling uncertainty. He had written, but hadn't seen, his grandmother since leaving Jamaica. His grandfather had died a few years ago, but he had not been able to get home for his funeral. He knew there was little work to be had in the countryside. He would likely have to go to the city to find work, but he was a country person at heart. He had seen just enough of Toronto to know that he didn't like cities.

I was on the verge of asking why on earth was he returning to Jamaica but remembered the look on his face when I asked him earlier about his time in Canada and decided to let it be. I picked up my book and started to read. Our plane would land in Kingston shortly.

As the plane taxied to a stop, I turned to him once more and asked a question I considered safe.

"How will you get to your village from here? It's a long drive from Kingston to your parish. Is a relative coming to pick you up?"

"I have a ride," he said after a pause.

It was time to get up. I started to gather my belongings. The young man sat still.

"You look very comfortable there," I said. "Aren't you getting up?"

Before he could answer, a flight attendant approached our seats and stopped, leaning over me to speak to the young man.

"Please wait till all the other passengers have left the plane," she said.

It sounded like an order, not a request.

"Thank you," he replied respectfully.

I stared at him, puzzled. He did not meet my eyes.

The line of passengers leaving the plane had come to a stop behind me. I hastily said goodbye, wished the young man "all the best," and then left the airplane, feeling a little sad.

My relatives greeted me with hugs and laughter. On the way to my mother's home, I told them about the young man.

"I had the strangest thought," I confided. "There was something missing from his answers ... as if he had been in Canada but hadn't really lived there ... as if he missed several years of his own life. Could he have been ..."

"In prison?" said one of my relatives, continuing with, "Yes. He's a deportee. They always leave the plane last. They get escorted out. We hear about them, young men who leave here as boys, full of hope, going to join their parents abroad. Then they commit a crime and end up in prison. When their time is up, they get deported. They're treated very badly down here. Nobody will hire them. They don't fit in anywhere. They fall in with the wrong crowd. Some get killed."

I am going home for good, he had said, but some people would see him as coming home for bad.

It would have been so easy for him to pocket my ring. It would have fetched him a good sum, money he clearly needed. Instead, he had returned it to me, as though that was only the right thing to do.

As we travelled on the winding Jamaican country road to my mother's home, I remembered a conversation from my teenage years.

"How come some people succeed, and some people fail?" I once asked my mother.

"Ah, m'dear," she replied, as though trying to figure it out herself, "parenting ... ambition ... education ... hard work ... discipline ... money ... choices ..."

Then Mama sighed and added one more thing to her long list.

"And grace. A lot of grace."

"Grace?" I asked.

"You can have all those things, do all the right things, and still fail. Sometimes, it's also about getting the opportunity and help you need, at just the right time. Grace."

I arrived at my mother's house to, as always, a scrumptious Jamaican meal. In her small dining room overlooking the green valley below, we bowed our heads and said grace before eating.

There it was again – grace. Some people call it luck, fortune, or fate, but Mama always called it grace.

I hadn't given it much thought before. Yet, what my mother termed grace had taken many forms throughout my life, from a mother who never stopped believing in me to a young stranger returning a precious ring. And, repeatedly, those moments of unexpected help, coming at just the right moment, had helped me to take one path when I might easily have taken another.

As the shadows lengthened and deepened on the mountainside and the air grew cool, the animals and birds quieted down for the night. After we got ready for bed,

I knocked at Mama's bedroom door, requesting a small favour.

Bringing back thoughts of the many times she and I had done this during my childhood, and thoughts of a young boy doing the same with his grandmother, we knelt beside her bed and prayed. For a young man whose name we didn't know, returning to a village whose name I had heard once, but immediately forgot. We prayed. That he might receive the opportunity to come home for good.

Chapter Twenty-seven

My Inheritance

Losing one parent had made Mama more precious to me; she now occupied an even bigger part of my heart.

For the first few days of my visit, we stayed close to home and each other. At least in the beginning, I didn't want to share her with anyone else, and she seemed to feel the same.

Wherever I went, inside or outside the house, I still expected to turn a corner and see my father, smiling his broad welcoming smile. I wondered if my mother had gotten used to the fact of his death yet, but I didn't ask. My mother always had her boundaries. I usually followed her cues when it came to discussing personal matters.

In the mornings we went for walks along the narrow, winding hillside road, she a few steps in front, me padding behind her like a duckling following its mother.

Impressive mansions, so much grander than my mother's home, lined both sides of the road. Mama said many of them were built by my former classmates.

"Trying to tell me something, Mama?"

She laughed.

Sometimes I tried to catch up, to hear what she was saying. But each time she told me sharply to fall back because the cars on this narrow road drove so fast that I might not be able to jump out of the way in time. I had long forgotten the road survival skills I learned as a child.

Back home, we sat on the verandah. The cool mountain breezes brought us the sweet, fragrant scents of flowers and lemon blossoms as we talked about our family's history. Birds sang all around us. Brilliantly coloured butterflies flitted from flower to flower, then sailed away to who knows where. A cow lowed in a nearby field. A goat bleated. A dog barked. A car tooted its horn in warning as it rounded a sharp curve in the road.

A secondary reason for my trip was to collect an ancient four-poster bed left to me by my cousin Ken, who had inherited it from his grandmother, my great-grandmother Eliza. But I had been tardy in collecting the bed – by years, not months. As far as I knew, it was still in the old family homestead, more than an hour's drive from my mother's home in the mountains.

If a bed can signify home – complete with love and family, comfort and security – it was that bed. Over the decades, generations of my family had lain in this bed. Some had been conceived and born there, some had fallen ill and been nursed back to health there, some had said their prayers there, some had dreamed and even died in this bed.

It stood proudly, massively in my great-grandmother's bedroom for as long as anyone could remember. The gleaming rich-brown posts and panels were a reminder not only of our matriarch herself, but also of the generations before and after her. I, and almost all my relatives, had slept or rested in this bed at one time or another, sometimes just snuggling into it for a moment of respite from the world. Big hands, little hands, rough hands, smooth hands – all at one time or other had rubbed the tall posts, savouring the smoothness of the dark, polished wood.

In these early days of my visit with my mother, the antique mahogany bed was never far from my mind, but I didn't mention it. I trusted my mother to tell me when the right time had come for us to collect my inheritance.

Occasionally, a neighbour passing on the road in front of my mother's verandah called a greeting. When that happened, she stopped her storytelling to ask a "how-de-do?" Sometimes, it took a long while before the answer was finished.

"... And horse dead and cow fat," I said, smiling, as the neighbour finally continued down the road. It's an old rural Jamaican expression, one that Mama often used to describe a rambling answer that never quite gets to the point.

We went on like this, warm and comfortable with each other, for four peaceful, restful days. Mama cooked. I washed the dishes and cleaned the kitchen. She told me stories from my childhood, stories from her life and the lives of her mother and grandmother before her.

The mention of my great-grandmother Eliza triggered the image of the bed again. I finally raised the subject, but my mother was in no hurry to discuss it. Instead, she asked out of nowhere "Did you know that you're the third child of a third child, of a third child, of a third child?"

I was surprised. I thought I knew almost everything about the family.

"No, I didn't, Mama. I knew that you and I were both third children, but I didn't realize how far back it goes."

"Ah ... well ... There's so much you still don't know, m'dear. You should know these things ... Did I tell you about that incident with Granny and the river, well over a hundred years ago?"

As my mother told Eliza's story, Eliza seemed to be right there, just a few steps from where we sat on the verandah. In fact, Eliza had spent the last several years of her life in my parents' home, and had often sat on this verandah, sharing her life story with her granddaughter, my mother Louise.

Eliza tried to force down her panic. Any moment now, the old rooster would start crowing, waking up the village. Quickly, she dressed her baby. The kerosene lamp was lit, the short wick giving just enough light for Eliza to retrieve her belongings without waking anyone else.

Eliza had been married for only two years. Her husband had fallen for her great beauty, ignoring the fact that his family already had someone else picked out for him: a young woman who was not descended from slaves. Although Eliza looked white, her African grandmother had been born into slavery. Somehow, the shame of slavery in Jamaica had ended up belonging not to the English who had profited from enslaving their fellow humans, but to the descendants of the Africans they had enslaved and forced to work on their sugar plantations.

Eliza's husband had made his own choice of bride, but it was Eliza who suffered because of that choice. He loved Eliza and their baby, but they lived in his parents' home and he found it very difficult to stand up for her against his family's criticisms. When he travelled on business, the family's treatment of Eliza ranged from unkind to downright abusive. One day, Eliza decided that she had to escape, to run back to her own family, even if just for a while.

Back in those days, when women had few legal rights, it was a huge decision for a married woman to leave her husband, even more difficult if she took their child with her. Both the law and the church would side with her husband. But Eliza's mind was made up.

Early one morning, when her husband was away, she slipped out of the house, cradling the baby on her hip. To get to her family home in another parish, Eliza had to walk for miles and cross a deep river. She had crossed it once before, but that was in daylight, with her husband helping her and the child. When she got to the river, she found stepping stones that she seemed to remember from the last time.

She was halfway across when she heard a shout.

"Don't move …"

Through the early morning mist a man ran down the river-bank toward her.

"Don't move!" he shouted again. "Stay right there!"

The man stepped carefully on the same stones Eliza had used and held out his hand. Somehow, she trusted him enough to take it. He led her back to the riverbank and pointed to the stone she'd been about to tread on.

"One more step," he told her, "and no one would ever have seen you or your baby again. Many a stranger has died, sucked under by the current, just swept away."

The man guided Eliza and her baby to another part of the river downstream, watched them cross safely, waved goodbye, and disappeared back into the mist.

A few years later, Eliza ended her marriage and met another important man – the man who would become my great-grandfather.

My mother stopped her story. After a long pause, she said, "My mother was her third child."

"Did anyone ever learn who the stranger was?"

"Never. Some people wonder if he was an angel, or maybe the spirit of an ancestor. How else do you explain that he walked out of the mist just in time, then simply disappeared?"

Chapter Twenty-eight

The Rebel Gene

The Jamaican sun shone hot every day, and every day my mother told me family stories. Sitting on the verandah, we travelled through the ages from her grandmother Eliza's life to her mother Artress's life and back to her own, often connecting the stories of all three women in one tale.

Their stories had the same elements: challenging times, high stakes, tough choices. Stories about strong, brave women in a Jamaican culture that breeds strong, brave women.

When I marvelled at some of the hardships they endured, the fights they fought and won, my mother responded with a familiar proverb: "What doesn't kill you makes you strong."

"So that's where the rebel gene came from," I said. "At some point in each of your lives, you had to go against the grain, to fight like crazy to survive."

"You come from a long line of rebels," Mama said. "Don't forget – your grandmother was the biggest rebel of all."

Artress had been just as determined as her mother Eliza. Born at the turn of the century, her legend began when she was just a young girl and discovered a mistake in the mathematics textbook used to educate primary school children in the British colonies. Because of her, education authorities in Jamaica wrote to their counterparts in England, and the mistake was corrected in the next edition.

The love of Artress's life was her intellectual equal, a brilliant inventor and goldsmith named Victor who kept inventing things way ahead of their time. His most memorable creation was a strange-looking vehicle that could carry six people. Unfortunately, local authorities refused to give him a licence to drive it on the road.

One rainy night, Victor fell on a wet pavement, hit his head, and died soon after, leaving Artress a widow with nine children. She supported them by working as a seamstress, then as a nurse at the local infirmary, and sometimes both.

She must have felt terribly vulnerable at times, but few people, including her own children, ever saw that side of her.

What hadn't killed Artress had made her strong. It had also toughened her and made her less patient with everyone around her.

No institution was too powerful for Artress to fight. She had no time for church rituals she considered foolish, like the practice of delicately sprinkling holy water on people's foreheads and declaring them baptized as children of God. If you wanted to be saved by God, she believed, you had to follow the practice of John the Baptist and get completely dunked in water, or it didn't count.

Turning away from the churches of the day, Artress helped to establish a tiny church in her village complete with a baptismal well under the floorboards of the altar platform. It was a church of plain language, heartfelt engagement with God, loud singing, and liberal doses of fire and brimstone. Not surprisingly, she became the church's deaconess.

In the early sixties, Artress helped to organize the union in the infirmary where she worked. There were furtive late-night union meetings and whispered plans with supporters in the family parlour. It was a volatile time in Jamaica's labour history, with unions controlled by Jamaica's two rival political parties, street gangs sometimes hired to fix the vote, and nervous employers everywhere.

All the while, Artress knew that at any moment she could be fired. She was suspended from her job at least once. But she kept on fighting.

My mother interrupted her story to say, "We were all afraid something terrible would happen, but she always felt it was the right thing to do."

All this had taken place during the years when we lived in my grandmother's house. Now I understood better why our grandmother had always seemed worried and upset, why she so rarely smiled. I was delighted that my mother, who suffered while living at her mother's house during that time, could speak about her now with such understanding and even pride.

Mama asked me, "Do you remember going to the infirmary?"

I nodded, and suddenly was seven years old again, a tiny creature in a cotton floral-patterned dress, thin sticks for legs and arms, thick reddish hair barely contained in two long braids.

No matter what battles brewed between Artress and the various authorities, there was one commitment that she and her daughter Louise never broke. Twice a week Louise's seven-year-old daughter – Artress's granddaughter – would be marched up to the infirmary to read the Bible and newspapers to the old and infirm folk who lived there. For most of these residents, the small child and her mother were their only visitors.

At first, the little girl didn't want to go. Who were these queer old people who had no relatives to call their own? Whose eyes seemed to devour her as she read to them? Then one day, as she read, she glimpsed her grandmother watching her from *the doorway, smiling so proudly it warmed her heart. She noticed something else, too. The moment she walked through the doorway, the eyes of the old people lit up and their wrinkled brown faces brightened into smiles.*

A strange thought hit me.

"Oh my gosh! I suddenly realized something, Mama! I started reading the news to an audience when I was just a little girl! No wonder I took to television journalism so easily. It never scared me at all."

Chapter Twenty-nine

Market Day and a Confession

One morning, my mother and I went to market. This market and I had a history, one that came flooding back the moment I started climbing the endless steps to its huge, dark entrance.

I was ten years old, had started high school months earlier, and now insisted on my right to a family tradition, that when you were old enough to go to high school, you were old enough to go to market by yourself on a Saturday ... old enough to buy the family's weekly supply of fresh vegetables, fish, and meat. It was a rite of passage.

That first Saturday of my growing up, I got no farther than the market entrance before I was trapped in a mass of other people's bodies. I was much too short to see where I was, or even where I wanted to go. The crowd moved, flowed, and surged, sweeping me along with it.

Everywhere around me were "higglers": people who farmed, or toured local farms buying up poultry, fruit, garlic, scallions, and yams to sell for as much as they could haggle in the market. Higglers lived by their wits and made room for nobody, not even a skinny ten-year-old girl who couldn't see above the crowds. The higglers shouted and shoved their way through the crowd, ready to trample me or anyone else who got in the way.

"Mama, do you remember that tall man," I began, reminding her of a market vendor who carried a big metal pot on his head and stormed his way through the crowd like Moses parting the Red Sea, shouting, "Hot water ... hot water ... coming through ... coming through ..."

My mother laughed and picked up the thread.

"And the crowd would have to part and let him through because he was so tall, nobody could see what he had inside the pot. We had to take his word and jump aside because we didn't want to risk getting scalded!"

How I wished I could become as tall and clever as that man! But at ten years old, I had to settle for another strategy, supplied by my mother.

"Start with a very determined look on your face," she instructed. "Like this!"

She scowled, looking very angry for a moment. "Then swing your arm back and forth and stick out your elbows. Like this! And if someone pushes you, just push them right back! This is not the time to be ladylike or say sorry. Just keep moving."

For days after this survival lesson, I marched around the house with what I believed to be a fearsome scowl on my face, elbows out, swinging my arms like a soldier on parade. I was convinced that I looked like a dangerous warrior.

Until the next market day.

Saturday came and brought with it my moment of truth. As I dutifully followed my mother's instructions, a huge higgler woman stopped moving. For a moment, she seemed to hold back the entire crowd.

"Lawd have mercy pon mi!" she cried out. She pointed at me in disbelief. "Anybody ever see a little pickney like dis? So lickle and so rude!"

Remembering my mother's advice, I forced myself to look the woman in the face, then made my way quickly past her and through the crowd.

It worked! It worked, it worked!

When I got home and told my mother, she howled with laughter, filled with pride at her ten-year-old "pickney," who, despite being "so lickle," had succeeded at being "so rude" that the higglers had let her pass.

~

Mama and I bought mangoes, bananas, tangerines, fresh fish, bammies (freshly baked cassava cakes), scallions, and thyme. It was like old times. Mama pushed her way through the crowd, elbows out, me sheltered in her wake. Then came the teasing, cajoling, and bargaining with the toughest merchants.

The next day was Sunday – my fifth day back in Jamaica. The four-poster bed was heavy on my mind, but still my mother hadn't mentioned it. Instead, she dressed for church. Like her mother before her, she was a deaconess, an important, powerful person in the village. I was a long-lapsed churchgoer, but there was no question in either of our minds: I was going to church with my mother.

I surprised myself with the realization that I was actually looking forward to the service. I missed the old folks, the old hymns, and the fiery sermons. I even missed the overriding sense of community I had chafed against as a teenager.

Our community certainly subscribed to the old African proverb that it took a village to raise a child. Village and church were simply different names for the same tribe. Misbehave in the village, and you would bring down the wrath of any elder who caught you. Misbehave in church (falling asleep, whispering, fidgeting, or worse, giggling during the pastor's sermon), and you'd feel the sharp prick of a relative's hatpin or the fierce glare of a nearby adult. Catch the pastor's attention more than once, and he might even work your disgrace into his sermon.

~

It was a tiny church when I was a child, modest and a little battered at the end of a rocky, potholed dirt road. Today the road was paved, and the building was grander and twice its original size. The church was full, just like it always was. Many of the women wore small netted hats perched stylishly on their heads. Three little girls wore frilly blue, yellow, and pink dresses, with pretty hair ribbons to match and bright white socks peeking above black patent-leather shoes.

I could picture my sisters and me, dressed much the same, trying to remember to sit up straight and act like well-behaved children. Now, in empathy, I smiled at the children and they shyly smiled back.

The choir, dressed in bright purple robes, slow marched down the aisle and up the steps to the loft. They led the congregation in a hymn I hadn't heard for more than thirty years. I surprised myself by remembering every word.

My mother, deaconess like her own mother before her, left her seat and walked to the front of the congregation, a strong, beautiful woman with silver-black hair cut fashionably short, wearing a confident and understated dress.

She told the congregation about upcoming events and poked fun at herself for mispronouncing a name. People laughed good-naturedly. This was our village. We were among friends.

I was fascinated by her ability to hold her audience. She didn't just read off a list of dates and events; instead she involved *everyone* in the life of her church. First, she called out a date. Next she declared that something important was set for that date. Finally, she called on different people to remind her what that something important was. Which meant that everyone in the congregation was quickly learning to keep track of events by themselves.

It was much safer than being embarrassed in front of the whole congregation.

In this church, my mother was leader, teacher, and friend, all at the same time. The thought made me tear up. I fished around in my purse for a tissue.

Louise and all of her siblings had been extraordinarily bright children. Louise was the third child and wanted, more than anything else, to be a teacher. It should never have been a problem. She was brilliant and worked very hard. But to prepare for the exam, she needed some high-priced textbooks, and her parents would have to pay the entrance fees.

Money was scarce, but, encouraged by her father, she believed the money would be found for her education.

Until Victor died suddenly. He had been both the bread-winner and her favourite parent: the father who made her laugh, the father who supported her dreams, the father who treated her as an adult, an equal. His death was a crushing blow to her, but there was worse to come.

Louise finished her studies, expecting to write the exams for teachers' college. That exam called for special preparatory text-books and fees. But there was no money. She repeated the final year over and over, all the while hoping this was the year her mother would find the money necessary for her to enter college.

Louise became an adult waiting for an opportunity that never came. She finally left school when she was twenty. She married a local boy and raised five children. Her fierce ambi-tions for herself were passed on to her children.

"Aim for the stars," she told them. "Work hard. Never settle for second best."

But every so often, her children felt her unspoken regret, that life hadn't turned out as she'd dreamed.

Her third child, the one who always pestered her with ques-tions, once asked her, "Why are you so sad, Mama?"

"Ah, m'dear ... What doesn't kill us makes us strong."

It wasn't the first time her mother had used the saying, nor the first time the child had felt an utter dislike for it.

The service was over, the congregation was slowly leaving, but my mother told me to stay. She and the other elders rose up from their benches and formed a circle around a young man who was sick. The pastor anointed his forehead with consecrated oil. The elders joined hands, and one by one, they prayed. Each picked up the prayer where the other left off.

As I stood there, I began to understand why people needed such rituals. The rituals connected them to one another. In so doing, they connected them to something bigger than themselves: their faith, their communities, their families, their common history. Ritual reminded them that they were all part of a wider, larger family. None of them was alone.

～

My visit was nearly over, and still we hadn't talked about my great-grandmother's four-poster bed.

Finally, my mother confessed. She had known for months that the bed wasn't in the old homestead any more. The distant relative who now lived in the house had given it away.

I was crushed.

My mother tried to explain. "You know ... There are some inheritances that we're better off without," she said gently, shaking her head. "Ah, m'dear. Try to understand. That bed ..."

She chose her words carefully.

"That bed has seen a lot of heartbreak and real tragedy. The people who slept in that bed had a far harder life than you can even imagine."

She took my hand and looked me in the eye, urging me to understand.

"You must make your own bed, m'dear ..."

I was not satisfied. I wanted more.

"What didn't you tell me about Granny's life? And her mother's life? What *were* the bad things?"

"Ah, m'dear."

Her voice was soft, sad, remembering.

"Sometimes, life is so terrible, it's all a person can do to stay alive."

After a while, her voice became strong again and her words positive, alive with hope.

"But with the grace of God, what doesn't kill you will make you strong enough to face tomorrow."

A chill went down my spine. But for the first time, I understood those words. I grasped the hope and faith, resilience and courage in a saying I had heard many times before but considered too grim to even explore.

Faith and hope, resilience and courage. They had seen my African ancestors through the brutalities of slavery: the beatings, the rapes, the dehumanization. And, in the decades that followed, they had seen my great-grandmother, grandmother, and even my mother through unspeakable events.

Suddenly, it was enough. I didn't need to hear any more.

On the flight back to Canada, I smiled at my mother's clever planning. She had deliberately saved the news about the bed until she was certain I had grasped a far more precious inheritance: my own family history. Day after day she had shared that inheritance through the lives of strong, brave women in a culture that, of necessity, has bred strong, brave women. They were the stories of the third children: my great grandmother, my grandmother, and my mother herself.

And yet, there was no avoiding it. Joy and sorrow, ugliness and beauty, tragedy and triumph sometimes shared the same bed. But the overriding story, the true gift, was one about people finding the strength to face tomorrow.

Part Four

The Blue House

If I were asked to name the chief benefit of a house, I should say: the house shelters daydreaming.

~ Gaston Bachelard

Chapter Thirty

Country Road

It's just past dawn when I open the side door of our small blue house in the woods, where we've been living now for nearly six years. Across the lawn, at the edge of a patch of woodland, Mindy, all glossy black fur and guilt, slinks away. On the grass below our bird feeder, grey and blue feathers are scattered on the grass.

Mindy is our neighbour's cat, and she has just dined on blue jay for breakfast.

I suppose it's our fault, really. Mindy believes that our home and grounds are hers – after all, my daughters and I have pampered her with treats since she was a kitten. But how were we to know that she'd grow up to be such a fearsome predator? She delights in chasing chipmunks, rabbits, and squirrels that gather – often, quite peaceably – under the bird feeder in our garden. And, when she can catch them, she kills and eats the birds.

I pick up my running shoes from their usual spot just outside our door. Before putting them on, I turn them upside down and shake them out. The last time I forgot to do this, my foot squashed a soft, cushy frog. My foot and I have never forgotten that sensation, and we're determined to never repeat it.

I grab my neon-green hand weights – bought at a

ridiculously low price because of their crazy colour – and head to the garden. Dozens of large white hydrangea flowers nod lacy round heads over a low stone wall that follows the curve of a long, serpentine garden bed. There are exactly six hundred and seventy-seven rocks of various shades, sizes, and shapes in that wall. I know this because I placed them there myself. It took me two years, and when I finally finished, the family opened a bottle of cheap champagne to celebrate.

To everything there is a season, a time for every purpose under heaven. Autumn is a busy time in the animal kingdom, each creature preparing for the change of seasons just ahead. Our resident chipmunks scurry about their business, pause to watch me, then go back to work. A black squirrel runs across the grass in front of me, stops to inspect the nut held in its front paws, sniffs it, then scampers off to wherever it stores food for the winter.

I turn left through the strip of woods that borders one side of our property. I stop for a few seconds to hopscotch on the large flat stones that Hamlin and I placed here to make a path from the garden gate. I feel entirely like a little girl back home in Jamaica.

A fragrant, late-flowering clematis vine runs along the dark wood of the old split rail fence. It almost covers the arbor over the garden gate before continuing along the other side. Its small cream-coloured blossoms make a charming contrast against the dark wood.

Opening the garden gate, I am only steps away from the narrow lane that leads to my house. On one side of the lane stretch hundreds of acres of dense forest. I've never made this walk without slowing down here to give thanks for the sheer *grace* of living in this place. It's a small slice of paradise. A never-ending landscape of woods, paths, streams, the occasional elusive whitetail deer, and all the birdsong a person can glory in.

When the sun goes down, legions of stars shine against the vast black velvet night sky. In our small paradise, nature is the star. The families who live around here have fought for decades to keep it this way.

These days, however, you can feel, taste, smell something in the air. Change is heading our way, and I know it will bring a whole new set of unknowns with it.

We've lived in bigger houses. But here, with no dining room, not enough closet space, small bathrooms – in fact, everything too small except the great outdoors – my family feels at home. We belong here.

Hamlin, our two daughters, and I can't get through the day without bumping into one another. When my mother visits, the house feels comfortably full, but never overcrowded. Occasionally, tempers flare, but no one locks away resentments or themselves for long. It's a house of love and hugs.

"Home, the spot of earth supremely blest, a dearer sweeter spot than all the rest," wrote Robert Montgomery. With its trees and streams and modest dwelling, this place reminds me of the country cottage we loved and lost and of my first childhood home in Jamaica.

It has also been my sanctuary, a refuge from a high-flying career in network television. Far from home, on one international flight or another, in one strange hotel room or another, in one foreign city after another, I can always close my eyes and summon up the images and sounds of the small blue house built thirty years before, nestled into the hillside. Sounds of family inside. Sounds of nature outside.

I hear the waterfall in the little stream that runs alongside the house, gurgling and splashing its way over rocks as it courses downhill to the larger trout stream at the back. I see the banks of ferns that share the sloping land, giving way to meadow rue, wild ginger, and a host of other perennials. I smile at the memory of the long, thin weeping-willow branches bending down to meet the water, engaged in some ancient ritual of the natural world.

"Change brings change," my mother always says. Much sooner than we expected when we moved in, development is already changing the local village. Fields that once sprouted corn and hay are now filled with very new, very large houses on very small lots.

Out of nowhere, it seems, subdivisions crammed with houses have sprung up, both inside and surrounding our village. That means many more cars. When we first moved here, our home was only an eleven-minute drive to the commuter train, which took forty minutes to reach downtown Toronto where Hamlin and I worked. Now, less than a decade later, as the number of city commuters multiplies, travel times have doubled. On some days, we spend a total of four hours in train and car, often arriving home to paradise tired and cranky.

It's the old story of the family that moves to what it believes is the last unspoiled place on earth – or at least within driving distance of the city – not realizing that thousands of other people will soon be doing the very same thing.

"Try to remember the kind of September / When life was slow and oh so mellow ..." I can almost hear the words of the great Harry Belafonte.

Gone are the sultry days of summer. On the forest side of the lane, the berries on a mountain ash tree are turning red, as are the plumes of wild sumac and the wild apples on low spreading trees.

I hang a right from the front gate, stride briskly up the lane, arms pumping, weights swinging. The air smells fresh and clean. Our country lane, at this end, is one of those little pockets of serenity that few strangers ever enter. You come here if you have a reason – or if you're lost. Houses here range from sprawling ranch bungalows to small dwellings like ours. They fit easily, some imperceptibly, into the woods.

I smile at Bill's beloved calla lilies standing magnificently tall and red in his front garden. Bill and Ginette were the first neighbours we met. A tall handsome blond couple, immigrants from the Netherlands, they proudly told Hamlin and me that they'd raised nine children in their three-bedroom house. We warmed to them immediately.

Bill took us on a tour of his basement workshop where he carved ornate wooden spoon-holders. I admired the workmanship and the low price and bought one as a present for my mother. Since then, I've brought back a silver spoon from every city where I've travelled, and my mother lovingly arranges them in Bill's spoon-holder.

These days, however, Bill has stopped carving. The Alzheimer's disease that was barely noticeable two years ago has advanced, making Ginette nervous when he leaves the house. The neighbours keep an eye out for Bill when he heads off for a walk-and-smoke in the acres of forest across the lane. Once he knew these woods like the back of his hand, but recently he's got lost there a couple of times.

Soon, Ginette, tells me, they'll have to leave here, go someplace else where Bill can be looked after properly.

Change brings change. I'm reminded of an Iroquois Confederacy belief that every change must be weighed by its impact on succeeding generations. A short walk into the forest, at the top of a ridge, the sign on the lookout tower announces that, twelve thousand years ago, in the time of glaciers, this was "the Iroquois shoreline."

Change on this scale boggles my mind. It's hard to believe that the waters of Lake Ontario, a twelve-minute drive from here, once stretched this far north.

On both sides of the lane, the wild cucumber vines are

in bloom. Their geometrically shaped leaves and frothy light-green blossoms scamper up the dense trees and tall shrubs that line the laneway. As one of the last vines to bloom, the wild cucumber is a harbinger of a harsher time ahead. Once the wild cucumber blooms, nothing can hold back the change to bitter cold weather and long dark nights.

I feel a sense of foreboding, as if – as an older relative of mine used to say – there's a goose walking over my grave.

The lane ahead is now a long ribbon of dust and gravel, flanked on both sides by green oceans of corn. You can tell, just by looking at the cornfields, whether we've had sufficient rainfall that summer. Last year, fields of yellow, defeated corn bordered this lane on both sides.

Out here in the country, where farmers get all or part of their living from crops, the life source for crops is sun, soil, rain, and snow. We homeowners get our water from wells, which depend on the same rain and snow.

A pickup truck heads down the lane toward me, stirring up clouds of dust. The driver slows and waves. I wave a neon-green weight back at him. He grins, and I grin back. If I'd been walking on a street in the village, we would have ignored each other. But out here on the country lane, there are certain conventions that must be observed. If you come across another human being – even in a pickup truck – you smile, wave, say hello.

I slow down in front of a long, tree-lined drive that leads to a red brick farmhouse and a huge grey barn and stables. This is where our fourteen-year-old daughter Lauren hangs out whenever she can. Because of the horses. She, like her older sister Nikisha before her, loves horses. She's been taking riding classes for a few years. At home, she sketches horses and dreams of having one of her very own.

Every day after school, Lauren and her friend Nicole walk up the dusty road to the farm. Lauren carries a plastic purple tack box packed with brushes, picks, and other items for grooming the horses.

Lauren's favourite horses, Victory Star and Lady, and the owners of the farm, are glad to see her each afternoon. Lauren, sometimes helped by Nicole, cleans the horses and stables at no charge.

When Lady was in foal, Lauren lived in a state of high excitement, giving us daily reports on the expectant mother. When Lady finally gave birth, you would have thought it was Christmas and Lauren's birthday rolled into one.

Just up the lane is a grand brick house surrounded by a barn, tall grain silos, and beautifully kept paddocks and fields. Horses and herds of placid cows graze in the sunlight. One of these years, according to the municipal plan, a four-lane highway will cut through here. I imagine the bulldozers and wrecking ball destroying everything and want to cry.

I walk to where our country lane is cut in two by the main road leading to the village of Brooklin. When we moved here, this was just another sleepy, country inter-section through farmers' fields. But now, on the far side of our gravel lane, lies a brand-new subdivision with big, new, two- and three-storey houses on plots only slighter bigger than the houses: long rows of them, crammed together as if Canada, the world's second largest country, is running out of room. A large man-made pond out front is supposed to make it all look rustic and natural. It doesn't.

I turn around, back the way I came. To my left, a herd of Jersey cows sprawl in a pasture. They too, will be gone by the time the highway comes through. But they are cows, and right now they seem totally content.

Whenever we come here together, Hamlin turns into a mischievous boy. He stops at the fence and bellows a low, convincing mooooooo. The cows get up clumsily, back legs first, and lumber toward him. Hamlin and the cows greet each other. He talks softly to them, some foolishness that I've never been able to decipher. The cows seem to understand, even if I don't.

We may roll our eyes at the endless, unrelenting development that encroaches on our country way of life and doubles our commuting time, but we also know that property prices have increased dramatically.

A neighbouring farmer, for one, is delighted.

"Look at it this way," he explains. "Farmers are always land rich and money poor. Most of us have farmed here for a long time and made very little money in spite of all our hard work. We start at dawn, keep going till it's too dark to do anything. It's been a very hard life. When we sell the land for development, we'll finally get enough money to retire and live a whole lot better."

It's the longest speech I've ever heard him make.

For us, the change is bittersweet. Our home sits on a few acres of land in the forest at the edge of the village. Developers could build more than half a dozen three-storey houses on it.

Every year the land becomes more valuable.

It's a Catch-22 situation. If we sell, we'll make a handsome profit, but we don't want to sell. Yet, with all the increased traffic and congestion, it's getting harder and harder to get to and from the city where we work and where much-loved relatives live.

"Development giveth and development taketh away." I have said this so many times in the last year that Hamlin sometimes finishes the sentence for me.

I walk back home along our country lane. Past the woods on my right and the trees and gardens and occasional neighours on my left. I give thanks again for my good fortune – that I've been given the incredible gift of being able to live in this paradise, this Eden.

As my mother says, change brings change. Soon, we'll have to make the decision to stay or go. But not yet. Maybe when the seasons change again, and the snow and bitter winds of winter have come and gone.

Chapter Thirty-one

Entertaining Angels

It was not faith that drew me, early one Sunday morning a couple years after we moved to the blue house, to the tiny old church in the village of Brooklin. Nor was I in the market for a spiritual home. No, it was curiosity, plain and simple.

I was drawn to the church by its timeworn white-board and batten exterior, narrow stained glass windows, gothic belfry, and welcoming front doors. Stepping inside, I saw simple wooden pews on both sides of a narrow aisle. Painted a nondescript shade of beige many years before, the pews were showing their age, as was the old red carpet that ran down the aisle to the altar. You could sense long years of worship here.

The worship space could probably accommodate about eighty people. But when I slipped quietly inside its doors for the eight-thirty service that first Sunday, just nine intrepid souls knelt in the pews. Every person could have had a whole pew, with lots of space left over.

The average age of the congregation seemed at least seventy, the average head of hair white. There was no singing of hymns. The language of the Book of Common Prayer – with its thee's, thou's, and spake's – seemed as archaic as the building itself.

One by one, the worshippers shuffled up the aisle to the communion rail. Hands outstretched in front of them, each received a piece of bread, then sipped communion wine from a silver chalice. I didn't join them.

Words from the Bible, words long forgotten, floated into my mind as I watched the worshippers: "Come unto me, all ye that labour and are heavy laden, and I will give you rest."

I could feel the worshippers' love for this place, their sense of belonging.

As the service ended, I headed quickly for the door, with no plan to return. But an elderly woman with greying light-brown hair and a sweet face approached me.

"Would you like envelopes?" she asked, touching my arm lightly.

It would have been like refusing your grandmother. And so, beating back a moment of apprehension, I accepted a small rectangular box of envelopes and told myself I could always drop them in the garbage when I got home.

"These are the remainder of someone else's envelopes," the woman said. "Our former minister, who left. Would you be comfortable using them?"

A strange question to ask, I told Hamlin later that day. And then I remembered hearing from someone in the village that the last minister had left the parish after a disagreement among the parishioners. Some had wanted to build a larger church to accommodate the growing population of newcomers flocking to the village. Others didn't.

Notwithstanding the friendliness of the envelope lady, this memory was enough to make me wonder if the people at this church had a problem with outsiders.

"That minister was the first woman priest at that church, and I seem to be the only black person there," I wailed to my husband. "Talk about being an outsider!"

In less than a minute, I had gone way past wailing and was now fast approaching the proverbial gnashing of teeth.

"And to make things worse, my envelopes are numbered 13! These are all *very bad* signs."

I was over-reacting, by any standards. I was in full-blown panic, and not sure why.

Meanwhile, I had taken the envelopes – envelopes for my weekly offering. What to do about them?

~

It was the kind of village you see on postcards, with old-fashioned main street, tree-lined roads, big houses with large verandahs.

The church stood on a corner. From the church, it was a short walk to the old village arena, where the country fair was held each spring, bringing loads of livestock, farm products, and people to the village. It was also a short walk to the brand-new subdivision, crammed with large houses designed to "fit in" with the older neighbourhoods nearby. Smack in the middle between the subdivision and the church, a farmer, who steadfastly ignored all the offers from developers who wanted to buy his land, still raised sheep.

When we were settling into our new home, we envisioned our first Christmas in the village: Christmas service at the church, hay wagon rides through the village, singing traditional carols. But life – and death – have a way of upsetting the best-laid plans. By that Christmas, we were grieving the deaths of two people we loved. Over the next two years came news of one death after another. When my beloved niece died unexpectedly, something withered inside me.

Mine had never been my mother's or grandmother's kind of faith in God, the kind that seemed to get even stronger during tough times. Mine had been a fair-weather faith, strong when things went well, shaky when things went off the rails.

Now, even that thin faith in God had gone, taking with it my oft-expressed belief that "things have a way of turning out well." I stayed away from church.

~

So what was I doing, two years later, visiting this church once and now twice? (There I was, the following Sunday, obeying an impulse I couldn't explain.)

Standing outside the small building, I finally noticed its name: St. Thomas' Anglican.

St. Thomas, patron saint of people who doubt, I thought. People just like me. I had always liked Thomas for honestly expressing his doubt about Jesus' resurrection from the grave. It would have been so much easier to pretend to believe, but "doubting Thomas" stood his ground until he saw his leader with his own eyes, and was invited to touch his wounds with his own hands.

He would have made a good journalist, that Thomas, I thought.

Once again, inside the church were only nine other people, all elderly. One of them was the envelope lady, who greeted me like the prodigal daughter returned. Her name was Gloria.

"Do you really have only nine people coming to this service?" I asked her.

"No," she said with a laugh and not a shred of embarrassment. "One Sunday we had only five!"

Admitting to a serious lack of customers is not usually a good idea, but Gloria's honesty was refreshing. She told me that the ten-thirty service, two hours later, was much more popular, packed full every Sunday. It had a Sunday school for kids and real, live music. The eight-thirty service, attended by people in search of something more contemplative notwithstanding, the church was fast running out of room.

~

That Christmas, the tiny church was packed tight despite the addition of two extra evening services and a whole lot of extra chairs. If sitting practically on top of each other made you irritable, it *really* helped to remember the story about the Son of God's birth in a barn because there was no room in the inn.

It was soon obvious, even to me, the newest congregant, that we needed a bigger church. I asked a few people about the space problem but couldn't get any real answers. In one case, a smartly dressed middle-aged woman gave me a rueful smile, made a quick excuse, and marched off to talk to someone else. If looks could talk, hers had clearly said: "Oh no! I'm not going down that road with you or anyone else!"

It was all very mysterious.

A new minister came to serve us. He must have been in his early thirties, but he looked much younger. What he lacked in age, however, he made up for with strong leadership skills, a pleasant manner, and a talent for getting things done. In no time, it seemed, a parish conference was held, and a Task Force on Growth was put together. People of all ages – from children to octogenarians – joined in a weekend retreat to face the future. It was a future in which our little village became a large, thriving town with a population more than quintupled.

Centuries ago, an apostle wrote the Letter to the Hebrews, which became a book in the Christian Bible. "Do not neglect to show hospitality to strangers," the writer urged, "for thereby, some have entertained angels, unawares."

Peter, the man who would become the first Pope of

the Christian church, went even further, telling the early Christians to "offer hospitality to one another without grumbling."

Perhaps remembering this admonition, the parishioners of St. Thomas' Anglican decided to open up the doors to their spiritual home – but only somewhat. They voted to hold an extra Sunday service to accommodate more newcomers.

Mention the thought of a bigger church and some parishioners actually shuddered. One old-timer seemed to sum up the general feeling, when he said, "No one has *ever* forgotten the baptismal font ..."

A painstaking history of the church, handwritten by an elderly parishioner, recalls how the church had once gone broke after using all its money to buy an impressive marble baptismal font. So broke that for two whole years, St. Thomas' closed down entirely. No services were held. Not on Easter. Not on Pentecost Sunday. Not on Christmas.

The church's history was a long, sad tale of problems, most of them financial. In 1879, only ten years after the building was completed, the parish had to borrow money to build a rectory for the minister "to relieve him of the burden of paying rent." That debt put the parish on a risky path.

Fifteen years later, despite "numerous socials at various homes," including a strawberry festival, a concert, and the sale of an expensive painting, the church was in debt up to its belfry and faced new calamities.

A report from the time reads: "Portions of the ceiling having fallen, the ceiling is in a dangerous state, from the bell and from the foundation of the chancel rising with the frost."

To add to the problems, the rector had rung the bell "with such gusto on New Year's Eve that it fell from the tower to the ground outside the church. The rector was pulled up to the ceiling by the bell rope and seriously injured."

I couldn't help grinning at the vision of the rector, doubtless a dignified and venerable example of his profession, being hoisted by his own bell rope.

"You'll go straight to hell for this," I told myself, still grinning.

All in all, for St. Thomas' Anglican, it was just one thing after another.

~

You had to look for it. But, hidden in all the church's calamities was a more uplifting narrative. The handwritten record shows a generation of "stout-hearted pioneers" who worked hard to keep the church alive. The women of the parish – though not allowed to be leaders or to even take part in church business except as "visitors" – played a huge role in raising money to help pay the parish debts. At the start of the twentieth century, it was also the women's group that held garden parties, organized concerts, and made quilts to raise cash for renovations.

Finally, in the 1950s, the church parish made the painful decision to sell the old church rectory, the one so lovingly built by parishioners in the late 1870s to provide their priest with a "convenient house" next door to the church. It was bought by Gloria, the church's much-loved "envelope secretary." It was understood that if she ever decided to sell, the parish would get right of first refusal.

A former churchwarden told me, "Everyone's hoping Gloria will hold off selling her house as long as possible," because the parish couldn't afford to buy it anytime in the conceivable future.

Chapter Thirty-two

Doubting St. Thomas'

By now, Hamlin and I had become regulars at the eight-thirty Sunday-morning service. We were warmly welcomed by the loyal congregation of older folk, particularly Gloria. She seemed to regard us as her own personal finds. Her eyes lit up the moment we walked through the doorway.

Without realizing it, we had become part of a caring community. If we missed a Sunday service, the priest or another parishioner called to make sure we were okay. If anyone in the family fell ill, someone called offering help or soup.

Then one day, right out of the blue, the priest came to visit our home, showing up in his white "dog collar," with his black priest shirt tucked into grey trousers. This, clearly, was no social call.

He came right out with it. Would I become a churchwarden?

I nearly choked. To be a churchwarden at St. Thomas' Anglican was to be one of two leaders both legally and financially responsible for the parish. And all the churchwardens I'd ever known were upstanding people of strong faith, like my mother and grandmother.

I felt like Alice falling down the rabbit hole, Dorothy

in the Land of Oz. I had to warn this man of God against his folly.

"I swear, you know," I blurted out. "I mean ... I use swear words ... sometimes."

The young priest smiled.

"I've used a few of them myself."

Taken aback, I threw my biggest weapon at him. The F-word.

"My faith is shaky."

There, it was, out in the open. No one would want a churchwarden whose faith was shaky. If this were the Wizard of Oz, I'd be a combination of the lion without courage, the scarecrow without a brain, the tin man missing a heart, and Dorothy without her red shoes. I sat back in my chair, confident that the priest would realize the error of his ways and we could all return to sanity.

"But your actions aren't shaky," he said, apparently unperturbed. "And your leadership skills are just what we need at this time."

I had run out of arguments. I found myself accepting the role.

The practical part of being a churchwarden – paying the bills, noting attendance, ensuring that repairs were made – was fairly easy, in part because my co-warden, Jack, was a marvel in these areas.

Even stopping my occasional swearing wasn't a problem.

Restoring my withered faith – a belief in God, or even the faith that things always work out – was a different matter. That called for a level of commitment I couldn't give at the time.

～

The congregation grew weekly. Even our eight-thirty attendance expanded. On a good Sunday, we sometimes hit fourteen.

Gloria, now in her eighties, was always there. But she was slowing down, her knees being the main culprit. Often someone had to help her up the steps to the communion rail. And as our small troop gathered for coffee after the service, the men playfully competed to be the one to bring Gloria her cup of coffee, knowing their antics would make her laugh.

Then came the day when Gloria fell down at home and broke her hip and had to be moved to the newly built seniors' home in the village. Of course, she had to sell her house, the old rectory. Was our parish willing to buy it, to return it to the church?

Turned out the parish was willing, but its purse was weak.

We had enormous problems. The priest and two churchwardens were all new to their roles. All three of us felt out of our depth. Overnight, the lovely dream of buying back the rectory had turned into the awful reality of having the opportunity, but no money to meet it.

Worse, we knew that the church had no choice but to expand in the future if it was to provide a spiritual home for the many newcomers arriving in our village. To expand the church, we needed to own the land surrounding the old rectory right next door.

Another Christmas, our busiest season, was approaching fast. It was clearly the wrong time to ask the parish to take on a huge debt of hundreds of thousands of dollars, especially in a church with financial anxiety in its DNA. We were on the verge of losing the old rectory, which one parishioner wrote "would be a body blow to the whole parish."

I appealed to the highest power I knew: my mother, once a church leader herself. Her wisdom, her faith in God, and her respect for the rightness of certain things were unassailable.

"Go talk to the people in your early morning congregation," my mother advised by telephone from Jamaica. "You know them. They know you. They won't let the three of you shoulder this burden alone."

Problem was, I didn't really know these folks. Coffee and a few laughs in the church kitchen after the service were one thing. Knowing them well enough to ask for big money was something else altogether. And those who claimed to know the eight-thirty folks well insisted they would be the last people at St. Thomas' Anglican to support taking on a giant debt to buy the old rectory.

"Mark my words," a longtime ten-thirty congregant told me in the tone of one-who-knows. "Those eight-thirty folks won't go for it. They're extremely conservative!"

Faith, a biblical writer had explained, is "the substance of things hoped for, the evidence of things not seen."

Mine was a small hope; my faith in these people was thin, shaky, full of doubt.

But mother knows best. So I visited the eight-thirty members who lived in the old village. I went from house to house, feeling tentative, uncertain, even fearful. When the first front door opened, I was still rehearsing my speech.

Their reactions astounded me.

One woman pledged a thousand dollars immediately. Her next words were stunning.

"I live on a pension," she said. "But my house is free and clear. Please use it as collateral on a mortgage or however it can be used. *I mean it.*"

Another woman and her husband listened attentively as I sat in the living room of their old clapboard house and earnestly described the challenge. When I finished, they calmly committed to a thousand dollars, promising more when they could afford it.

Even more remarkable, the woman fiercely urged us to have faith in the parish.

"The moment you've told people how much you need, they will open their wallets," she said.

She was right.

The money started coming in. Slowly at first. Then, as we persuaded the larger congregation to join us, faster and faster. Contributions ranged from a few dollars to several thousand. A young child gave a dollar – all the money he had in his piggybank. We were all deeply moved by the sacrifices people were willing to make to help their church.

Nobody mentioned the font.

Two weeks before Christmas, we had nearly forty percent of the purchase price. Three parish families agreed to take out mortgages on the property, and the diocese provided a guarantee to the lenders. And to our great joy, our offer to buy back the old rectory was accepted.

Finally, the old rectory was coming home, bringing with it an unspoken promise: more newcomers would find hospitality at St. Thomas', a place where their spirit could feel at home.

I stood with my mother, my husband, my daughters, and fellow parishioners that Christmas in St. Thomas' Anglican and my heart soared with happiness.

The whole church seemed to hum with new hope, faith, and hospitality. For old-timers and strangers – and any angels who might drop in unannounced.

Chapter Thirty-three

The Grandmothers Have Spoken

Our daughter Nikisha and her boyfriend, Tim, invited us to lunch in downtown Toronto.

"What do you think this is about?" Hamlin asked as we drove.

"I have no idea," I said. "Maybe they just wanted to invite us to lunch."

But I was wondering, too.

Nikisha and Tim had been dating for more than a year. Now, there was no question about it, they had been getting closer and closer. Nikisha had taken to bringing Tim home for Sunday suppers, and over many meals, Hamlin, Lauren, and I (and Mama when she visited us) had decided that we liked him.

They seemed a good match, we said behind their backs. Whenever Nikisha got overly serious, Tim seemed to know how to make her laugh. Nikisha was a good cook, a talent no doubt passed on from Hamlin and her grandmothers. Tim, meanwhile, seemed just about capable of boiling water. Nikisha tended toward ironic overstatement. Tim tended toward ironic understatement.

Now, over a nice lunch, I noticed that Tim looked nervous and Nikisha was slightly tense.

Turned out that Tim had chosen the old-fashioned

way of declaring his honourable intentions to the parents of his beloved. He and Nikisha had decided that they loved each other and wanted to seek our blessings on the relationship.

We gave it without hesitation. We already liked and admired this smart, pleasant young man, and we thought he and our daughter were good for each other. We said so now in a blabbering kind of way.

They sat still, waiting. It dawned on us that more was expected. As Nikisha's parents, we had a part in this ritual. But what? We felt as though we were being given a pop quiz and were screwing it up royally.

Indeed, Hamlin's only experience in this area was when he had gone, decades before, to introduce himself to my parents in Jamaica and declare his intentions. Perhaps my mother had been just as stuck for an answer, because her first words shocked Hamlin.

"That one is a rebel," she said. "Do you know that?"

Now *we* were the parents. And there were our daughter and her beloved, sitting across the table from us, anxiously waiting for us to say something, ask something.

I have no idea what questions we asked, but I know we asked them fervently, hoping all the while that we sounded like very responsible parents.

Neither of us remembers how they replied to our questions, but we found ourselves foolishly happy – over-joyed, even – with all their answers.

Tim later confessed that he was "sweating buckets" through the entire lunch.

"You two together are a daunting couple," he remarked. "Especially when you're asking tough questions."

Tough questions? We didn't know whether to be flat-tered or amazed, but we got the feeling that Tim and Nikisha approved. Still, Hamlin and I resolved to be more supportive and less intimidating in the months ahead.

~

The engagement party was held in our garden, with family and friends. It was a glorious day. The young couple's joy spread through the gathering, as people sat at cloth-covered tables under colourful umbrellas, or under the vine-covered rustic gazebo that Hamlin had made from fallen logs the year before, or under the shade of trees. Even butterflies and hummingbirds seemed to slow their flitting motion in the garden that day, as if tipsy with happiness.

After that, there was a wedding to plan, but Nikisha and Tim took charge. Both were outstanding project managers at work, and they proceeded to design and carry off the wedding plans calmly. Hamlin and I observed them with astonishment and pride. It became even clearer to us what a strong partnership these two young people had already forged.

"Would you be willing to take on this part?" they would ask family members, making sure we understood their vision and expectations.

It was to be a small wedding with fewer than a hundred persons. It was to be held at the downtown church they attended.

One thing I knew from early on: Nikisha's wedding dress would contain no frills. I thought she said this part with particular emphasis, as if she thought I might argue, but it made the search easier. Off we went, excitedly, to buy her wedding dress.

One of the few hitches in the wedding plans came from me. I was so completely focused on Nikisha and Tim that I completely forgot to buy a special dress for myself.

My project-manager daughter allowed herself to be briefly stunned before saying, "Mom! You can't just wear any old dress to my wedding. You're the mother of the bride!"

Then she hauled me off to a fancy store to buy an appropriate dress – just days before the wedding – and seemed unfazed when I bargained the price of the dress down by fifty per cent.

~

It was a beautiful wedding. Standing in front of the altar of the grand but somehow intimate old Anglican church in downtown Toronto, Tim and Nikisha pledged their love and commitment to each other, as family members and friends alike shed tears of joy.

Now downtowners, now part of a church that also ministered to street people, the bride and groom wanted the pictures of their big day to reflect a downtown sensibility. Photos were taken inside and outside the church, at the Royal Ontario Museum across the street, and on the street itself. When a drunken homeless man came to chat with them as they posed for photos on a bench, Tim, Nikisha, and the photographer all took it entirely in stride.

"It's all part of the downtown reality," they later explained. "And he was a nice man."

Hamlin and I were every bit the proud parents. Ours was a heart-swelling joy. We alternated between smiling, wiping away the tears, and reaching out to pat each other on the shoulder or on the arm. Lauren, who served as a bridesmaid, grinned through much of the ceremony, every bit the proud sister. But it was the grandmothers who stole the show.

Tim's grandmother, looking much younger and more stylish than any other eighty-something, beamed her joy to everyone. Both Mama and Hamlin's mother, Merle, gave speeches blessing the couple, the wedding, and the entire gathering. They did it with love, grace, and humour.

"There you have it," a relative nearby remarked with

a broad smile. "The grandmothers have spoken! This marriage will work out brilliantly."

Our cup of joy was full and running over. As a family, we had enjoyed many happy times, but this was, without doubt, one of the most joyful of all.

Chapter Thirty-four

Reconnecting

I had lived an adventurous life. Now I was living peacefully with my family in our little blue house in the countryside, one daughter happily married, the other finishing up high school, my mother visiting us from time to time.

Hamlin and I had both left our jobs in TV news a few years earlier, in 2000, and started our own management consulting firm, which was doing very well.

It was a good life, and I never took it for granted.

The contentment I felt was evident in my domestic life. For the first time, I looked forward to cooking. Not the kind of cooking I had done before – meals rustled up primarily to stave off hunger – but cooking for the enjoyment of my family. I liked the feel of combining ingredients in a bowl with my hands, the smell of mingled spices, the way the dish looked when it was cooked, the smiles of enjoyment on the faces of my loved ones.

I even started baking. Not cakes – perhaps I was still haunted by the charred, black mess of cake my grand-mother and I had tried to bake when I lived in her home – but muffins, particularly spiced apple muffins, which our family always devoured mere minutes after they came out of the oven, spilling forth the smell of apple and cinnamon.

One afternoon, on one of those summer days where the rain is inexplicably falling while the sun still shines and the raindrops are warm on the skin, Hamlin issued a dare.

"Bet you can't take off your clothes and go running in the backyard!"

I was a grown woman, not taken to running around naked, but he had said the magic words – *Bet you can't …* – and I was a child again.

This wasn't a taunt to climb a tall tree, or wade through a dark, water-filled culvert under a road, but it was just as irresistible. In no time at all, we both shed our clothes and went streaking, "bare-assed naked," as we later referred to it, all the way down the long backyard. Hamlin laughed and I shrieked with childish glee.

It helped that our home was almost entirely surrounded by woods and streams, with a forest for a neighbour. We delighted in long walks in the deep woods, especially in the fall. We kicked up the gold, scarlet, and russet-coloured leaves, or crunched them underfoot as we slowly meandered along paths lined by maple, oak, and white birch trees.

Our dog Kinu, an Akita with a big friendly face, huge furry body, and a tail with a double curl, seemed to take equal pleasure in these slow autumn walks through hundreds of acres of forest. He stopped to sniff leaf after leaf, and we let him, without complaint.

～

One late autumn day, as I sat in the living room gazing into the fire, giving thanks for the abundance of good things in our family's life, an image came into my mind. The face of a woman I hadn't thought about in years. Aunt Pat.

My mother had always been close to her aunt, uncle, and cousins on the Chinese branch of our family, and had remained especially close to two of her cousins throughout their lives. One was Mama's cousin Ken, the other was his brother Clan. Clan married a woman named Pat, and we children called them uncle and aunt. They had three young children.

During my early adolescent years, while we still lived at my grandmother's home, Mama had seen my frustration and decided I needed to get a break from life in our small village. So she and Ken conspired with Clan and Pat to send me to their home in Kingston, the big city of Jamaica, for weekends and part of every summer.

Every Sunday morning when I was with them, we visited bustling Barry Street in downtown Kingston to shop for food. The stores, presided over by old Chinese men and women, all smelled awful. In other words: wonderful, intriguing. Those smells transported me to other places, other lands, and other times.

As my aunt and uncle roved from store to store, choosing fresh vegetables, fresh shrimps, Chinese spices, and pungent sausages, I wandered the stores, inspecting their mysterious contents and striking up conversations with the shopkeepers.

Sometimes, in their mixture of English, Jamaican patois, and Chinese, the shop owners answered my questions about the ornaments they sold, the preserved duck eggs kept in big old clay jars, and even the sour plum candies for sale. I wanted to know everything. About China, about themselves, about how they had made the long journey to Jamaica.

Sometimes, tired of my endless questions, they shooed me away, turning to help their customers, or telling me that I was just too nosy for my own good.

"Time to go!" my uncle would call at last, as I lingered

inside a store he and the rest of the family had left at least three shops earlier. Sometimes the old Chinese shop-keeper laughingly thanked him, relieved to be rid of me.

Chinese culture had seized my imagination. My closest link to it was Aunt Pat's father, who had immigrated from China decades before and married a Jamaican woman but had remained very Chinese. He became the only grand-father I had ever known; my own grandfathers had died long before I was born.

He and his wife lived in a small house in Kingston, with a huge mango tree out front. Inside their house were Chinese paintings, Chinese ornaments, which hung in doorways, Chinese books and newspapers, and, always, the smell of Chinese food.

Through Grandpa, I became the only child in the family who developed an ardent appreciation for Foo Gah, the bitter Chinese melon stuffed with meat. If Grandpa liked it, it was good enough for me.

Every weekend, Grandpa taught me another few Chinese words. He taught me to count properly in Chinese, to understand the strange Chinese alphabet and words, and why the text in the Chinese newspapers had to be read up and down, not from left to right across the page as in English ones.

But the person I loved most in that family was Aunt Pat. At home in our village, my mother was kept busy raising five children, overseeing the building of the house, and managing her dressmaking business. She was glad that I was in good hands during these weekend visits. Indeed, Aunt Pat took it on herself to inform me that I was becoming a young lady, which meant that I needed to take better care of my hair, my body, and the way I dressed.

She liked skirt suits and sometimes bought enough fabric for her dressmaker to make two: one for her, the other for me. My first suit was made from thick cotton, with a blue and pink paisley pattern. She also took me to the hairdresser, who trimmed my long bushy hair, and taught me how to care for it.

I was growing up, becoming a young woman of sixteen.

I still had strong opinions. It was the late sixties and Jamaica was trying to find its way forward as a newly independent country. Jamaica was a cauldron of great hope, anticipation, and, simmering underneath it all, anger over divisions by colour, shade, and economic class. Attitudes toward foreigners, whites, and light-skinned Jamaicans were changing. Many had long enjoyed unearned privileges in a society where light skin was desirable, dark skin not. They were given the better jobs in the banks and other companies and were accorded more respect than others.

The Chinese-Jamaicans, even those born in Jamaica, now owned many of the shops and supermarkets. Some Jamaicans saw them as having gotten wealthy on the backs of African-Jamaicans and accused them of being prejudiced.

Dark-skinned Jamaicans were rebelling against those who mistreated them and those they only suspected of doing so. I understood their complaint. Many of my relatives were dark-skinned, and I heard their stories about the ways in which they'd been disrespected in their own land.

But I had also become close to my Chinese relatives, and had a better understanding of Chinese-Jamaican life than most people I knew.

It seemed that I was forever fighting on behalf of one side or another, and sometimes both at the same time. I came by it honestly: my mother and grandmother never let a negative comment about any race pass uncontested. But at sixteen years old, despite my intelligence and my way with words, I had none of the emotional sophistication required to navigate a terrain that was becoming more difficult by the week.

Then, one weekend, a Chinese friend of my aunt and uncle said a terrible thing about black Jamaicans. I turned to look at my relatives, expecting them to counter the repugnant remark. No one said a word.

When a similar incident happened weeks later, with the same result, I was crushed. Something shifted inside me, but I didn't know what it was. Days later, I realized that I had made a decision.

There would be no more weekends, no more summers, with my aunt and uncle.

I never returned. I never saw them or my beloved young cousins again. Never went to visit Aunt Pat's parents, never sat and learned how to read the Chinese newspapers with Grandpa. Never went to Barry Street. Never entered my relatives' house again.

It was one of those hurts that I locked away in a small part of my heart. Not forgotten, but also not reopened. Until now, years later, while living contentedly in the little blue house in the Canadian countryside.

Just a few months before, I had been introduced to an e-mail community of Jamaicans. I joined it and discovered within weeks that almost everyone else was of Chinese ancestry.

One day, while others extolled the beauty of their homeland, one woman revealed that she had never gotten over the trauma of leaving Jamaica.

"Why?" someone asked.

"What trauma?" someone else inquired.

It was the early seventies, she replied. She had felt driven out of her own country, rejected and disowned by other Jamaicans, all because she was Chinese by ancestry.

A flurry of emotional replies went back and forth between members in Canada, the US, and Jamaica, all reliving their memories of that time.

The time they spoke of was just a few years after I had

turned my back on my aunt and uncle and their family. Now, for the first time, I was hearing another side of the story, and understanding it in a new way.

I tracked Aunt Pat down within days. Now divorced from my uncle and living in the US, she had remarried and her children were now grown. She asked me twice to confirm who I was.

'I can't believe you're calling," she said, over and over. "You just disappeared."

We shared some memories of the old days, and when we'd finished that, she explained her decision to leave Jamaica and to divorce her husband. She talked about her experience as a single parent, about the tricks she used back then to stretch food supplies from one day to the next. She told me about some of the discrimination she had faced in her new country, being a Jamaican immigrant, a single mother, and a woman of colour in a mostly white environment. She was very proud of the times she had stood up to defend herself and other people of colour.

"Tell me everything," she said. "About your life, your family, your career. Tell me everything."

I tried to sum up a whole life in a few minutes on the phone. Told her about my family, my adventures, the projects I had led in Canada, Europe, and South Africa. The national and international awards that followed, including one received only months before: an award for outstanding achievement in Canada's film and television industry.

She rejoiced at how well I'd done.

"I owe a bit of my success to you, you know," I said softly.

"To me?" She sounded surprised.

"Yes. You helped build my confidence when I was an awkward teenager."

She thanked me, with a great deal of feeling.

Back then, I had expected her to understand why I was hurt. I didn't know how to describe the enormity of my own disappointment. So I had fled. Now it was time to try again, but this time, to also say something different.

"I love you," I said. "And I'm sorry. For walking out all those years ago, and for never getting in touch again. I'm very sorry."

"I'm sorry, too," she said, after listening to me explain what had happened. "But I wish you'd talked to me. I wish you'd talked to me about it, told me how you were feeling. I never understood why you left. Never."

~

Several months after that telephone conversation, Aunt Pat and her older son sat at the kitchen table in my family's home, the little blue house. Her hair was a little grey now, and her features had softened with age, but her laugh and keen eyes were the same. She remembered some things vividly, but admitted frankly that she had completely forgotten others.

The racial incident that led me to flee her home was one of them. I had been shocked during our telephone conversation to find that Aunt Pat had forgotten it, this thing that had become one of the defining moments of my adolescence. What she clearly remembered on the phone and again now in my kitchen was her sense of confusion and loss over my departure, but not what had triggered it.

Every so often, we reached out to touch each other's hands. In my home, far away from what had happened in Jamaica, my aunt, her son, and I relived the happy parts of our lives during those years.

Grandpa and his newspapers. The shopkeepers on Barry Street. The "thousand year old" duck eggs. The smell inside the Chinese shops. The times I'd climbed the mango tree, with Grandma anxiously yelling from the verandah below, "Come down right now! If you break your neck, your parents will kill me!" She never quite accepted my assurances that I wouldn't fall because I was an expert tree climber.

Hamlin sat, silent, shocked at these revelations. I had never talked about these years. He didn't know how closely I had bonded with this branch of my family, the time I had spent in their homes, and my close experience of the Chinese-Jamaican community itself. Nor had he known that I had simply walked away from people whom I loved.

"It's not like you at all," he said later. "That sounds like such a tough thing to do."

Indeed it was. Though I never talked about it, the memory of this brutal rending would have an impact on my behaviour in later years, along with memories of other actions: my rudeness to my father when he returned from England, having to revise my harsh opinion of my grandmother, my time with Miss Claire, and my mother's acts of forgiveness whenever I stepped out of line.

Sometimes the road to heaven is paved with angry intentions. All these events had taken place within two years of my adolescence, but they, like fire tempering glass, helped make me a more patient adult.

I took Aunt Pat's arm as we went outside for a short stroll on the grounds of my home. I showed her our family's favourite spots. The trail where Nikisha walked our pet dog Kinu, even now, on her visits home. The big white cedar, where Lauren's tree house perched overlooking the wetlands and both streams. The garden shed that Hamlin had converted into a small studio for writing or listening to loud music. My own favourite place where the little stream became a waterfall just before coursing down the slope to merge with the large brook.

We had missed whole decades, this woman and I. But

here we were, both grown women, in this peaceful home, at a precious time in both our lives. We fell silent, awed by this moment of grace.

Aunt Pat looked around the grounds, at the house, and at my face, as if committing them all to memory. And then she smiled and squeezed my hand.

~

In the weeks that followed the visit, I remembered the photographs that Aunt Pat had given me when I was a teenager. They were still in my old photo albums at the back of a cupboard.

A small black-and-white photo with scalloped edges showed a beautiful young woman on her wedding day, full of hope and grace. In another photo, she was wearing shorts and T-shirt, fiercely returning a volley from her opponent in the final match of a national table-tennis competition, which she went on to win. Aunt Pat had given me the table-tennis photo as motivation. Like her, I played the game competitively as a teenager.

I copied the photos and mailed them to her. Aunt Pat's three children reacted as if they had won the lottery. Indeed, memories were particularly important to them right then.

"She may ask you the same thing more than once," her son Paul had warned me before their visit to our home in Canada. "Don't worry about it. Just answer again."

Indeed, she had. And each time, I had lovingly repeated the answer I'd previously given, as if for the very first time.

But the signs were obvious. Aunt Pat's disease, Alzheimer's, was gaining strength. Within a year, it had taken over.

Chapter Thirty-five

Red Brick House Redux

The e-mail from Nikisha appeared in our inbox early one evening.

"Mum and Dad: Please have a look at the third house on this list. Does it look like our first home?"

We looked, and looked again. It was. We gaped, stared, then scrutinized the small photo of the front of the house, looked at each other, and yelled, "It is! It is!"

Nikisha and Tim had seen about sixty houses in the nearly two years since they'd been married. They'd even put in bids on some of them, but in Toronto's hot property market, they had been outbid on all.

"We're calling it quits for a while," they had said. "We're not up for any more rejections right now. Maybe the market will cool down a bit later on and we'll stand a better chance."

A sensible approach, we had said at the time.

But now the old house we had sold nearly two decades before – Nikisha's childhood home – was back on the market.

Hamlin calmly e-mailed back: "Yes, it's our old home. Wanna go see it?"

"I thought of it," she replied right away. "But I don't think I could stand being outbid on my childhood home. It would hurt too much."

Her father thought about it and pushed back. "You can still see it, sweetheart. Doesn't mean you have to buy it. We'll go with you for support."

As usual, he was the one being logical, while I was the one holding back, wanting to think harder about this, wanting to protect my child from disappointment. But I sensed Nikisha's interest in seeing the house, and I had also glimpsed the gleam in my husband's eye: he was curious about what the house looked like today. Visions of the kitchen he had ripped apart and rebuilt danced in his head. What other renovations had subsequent owners made?

Our son-in-law was also eager to see the home where his wife had spent much of her early childhood. With his encouragement, Nikisha made the appointment.

"My parents will be there to provide moral support for both of us if needed," she reassured Tim, perhaps knowing that she was really reassuring herself.

We arrived at the house, eager to look around but trying our best to appear calm. In the years since we sold it, relatively little had been altered. The sturdy wood floors and natural wood trim were immediately familiar. The kitchen was the same except for the fact that the current owners had painted the cupboard doors white and installed a larger window facing the garden.

Hamlin looked around approvingly. This was the kitchen that he had proudly installed, after "taking the walls down to the studs" and discovering, behind the plaster and lathing, that the room's only insulation consisted of seventy-year-old newspapers.

Downstairs in the basement, and upstairs on the second floor, new washrooms had recently been installed.

Nikisha and Tim admired the new sinks, tub, shower, and faucets, and the large-tiled surfaces of the floors and walls, and Nikisha noted that both washrooms were several notches up from our old bathroom.

Hamlin and I decided the best strategy was to look supportive but stay mum. After all, we weren't the home-buyers. Equally important, we did not want to contribute to any raised hopes, just in case. We would offer no assessments until requested by our daughter and son-in-law.

But Tim could hardly contain his pleasure. "This house ticks all our boxes," he said. "It has all the things we wrote on our list."

As he spoke, my husband and I scrutinized our daughter's face: it seemed to us that she was doing her best to hide her own delight. Just in case.

A day later, Tim and Nikisha went off on a planned holiday, leaving the real estate agent and us to handle the purchase offer. Although Harry had retired some years earlier, we were in excellent hands. Rosalee was different from Harry in some ways, reassuringly similar in others. Like Harry, she was clever. She registered the offer first thing in the morning, not waiting for the deadline. Since our family knew the house, we agreed that there was no need to wait for an inspection.

Then we sat back, bit our fingernails, and watched the minutes go by. Very slowly.

Finally, that night, we called Nikisha and Tim in Cuba to break the good news: the offer had been accepted. They had just bought their first house, by a minor miracle the house where Nikisha had spent her early childhood.

Tim and Nikisha moved in a few months later. Their belongings were relatively few. Hamlin and I had given them our old oak dining set as a wedding present. Now they proudly placed the table, chairs, and sideboard in the dining room, each piece of furniture returning to the same spot it had occupied when our family had lived in this house.

The timeworn antique pine chest – another gift to the young couple – also returned to its place of honour in the small living room where it once again served as a coffee table.

But then a strange thing happened. The moment all their belongings were put into place, the house transformed itself into Nikisha and Tim's home. It was no longer the old family home.

Just a few months later, they held their first family gathering in the back garden: a birthday party for my mother. Celebrating her birthday in a house that had miraculously come back into our family seemed like a double serving of grace. It was a day when the very heavens seemed to smile on our family.

Chapter Thirty-six

A New Church

All the while, the village of Brooklin near the blue house kept growing. Row after row of new houses was being built. More and more people were leaving the nearby cities and making their home in the village.

Over at St. Thomas' Anglican, we were running out of room fast. It was time to build the new church. Long meetings worked their way into the night. An architect and builders were chosen. Designs were drawn up and, after much discussion, approved.

The designer was Elizabeth Davidson, great-granddaughter of architect Henry Langley who designed the original church building way back in the 1860s. No one could figure out how a small country parish back then had managed to snag such a distinguished Canadian architect. Now, parishioners marvelled that his granddaughter was designing the new church, chalking it up to yet another piece of divine intervention.

The capital committee set an ambitious fundraising goal. People met in the hallways before or after the service and said they hoped we could meet the goal. Hamlin and his co-chair, Frank, were convinced that they could. The rest of us prayed that they would be proven right.

And then the parishioners swung into action, repeating

some of the fundraising methods of all those decades before. Jo announced that she would make a quilt and invited parishioners to buy squares in thanksgiving for their loved ones. Sharon put an antiques sale together and auctioned off an impressive number of valuable pieces. Annette planned a dinner dance. Parishioners visited one another in their homes. Funds were pledged. Ken, Peter, and other members worked hard on the design and construction phases of the project.

The committee exceeded its original fundraising target by fifty percent.

Six years after we'd bought back the old rectory, the people of St. Thomas' Anglican celebrated their first Christmas in a brand-new church. You could practically see a haze of pride emanating from them and wafting through the church.

~

The new space could shelter more than three hundred worshippers, four times more than the old one. It was an inspiring mixture of traditional and modern. Huge wooden buttresses soared into high ceilings. Light poured in through gloriously huge and clear glass windows. The music from the grand old organ that once graced a church in Quebec flowed through the sanctuary, filling it right up to the rafters.

Our former priest moved on to a bigger parish, having led St. Thomas' with distinction. We tempered our tears with the hope that God would send us "the right person." A search committee chose a new priest with the necessary gifts and talents to lead us through this next stage in the life of the parish. She became only the second woman priest in the history of the parish and the first African-Canadian. Within months, it felt as though she had always been among us.

And yes, the new building had a baptismal font. This one was impressively modern, with enough room for parishioners to be baptized while standing if they wished. Already, scores of babies and a few adults were baptized, welcomed into "the body of the church."

Watching the first baptisms, one old-timer slyly whispered that the font's best feature was that it came at a reasonable price.

"This one won't bankrupt the church," he whispered with a knowing grin.

~

Overnight, the old church took on a new identity as "the chapel," but it remained the place where the eight-thirty congregation worshipped. Not everyone understood why we stayed there. Not when there was a lovely, brand new church just across the hallway. Onlookers saw the battered old pews, walls that clearly needed another coat of paint, a carpet threadbare in spots, and the overused clothbound prayer books, some missing several pages.

For us, though – the eight-thirty folks – the timeworn sanctuary with its antiquated charm was a holy place, a refuge from life's cares. There was tenderness in our voices like that reserved for a precious family home when we talked about this old church.

And, somehow, the words in the battered prayer books were even more impressive to us because they were evidence of more than a hundred years of people's faith in God and love for this place. To us, there was surpassing beauty, a divine mystery, in the centuries-old Book of Common Prayer, still used in the eight-thirty service.

"Lift up your hearts!" the old book challenged us on days when our souls felt weary. On days when life seemed punishing, the prayer book reminded us of God's "favour and goodness toward us," that we are "living members of his mystical body," and "heirs through hope" of "an everlasting kingdom."

~

My own faith was an on-again, off-again affair, a slight improvement on having no faith at all. I wished I could be like the other people around me, one of "the blessed company of all faithful people." I wasn't there yet.

Still, as the sun streamed through the stained-glass windows and poured into our small sanctuary, my voice was always stronger as I considered a God who, "not weighing our merits, but pardoning our offences," understands that some people – like the disciple Thomas – need more time to figure things out.

As time went by, our eight-thirty congregation got even smaller. We lived through a sad season of bereavements, losing some of our most beloved members. Jean, who had written the historical account of the church's earlier years by hand. Gloria, the envelope secretary who had sold the rectory back to the parish. Joy, who had offered her house as collateral. And George, who had made one of the very first pledges. None of them lived to celebrate that first Christmas in the new church, to see the splendid result of our shared dream.

We remembered them at St. Thomas' Anglican. The old rectory, now the church office, was renamed for Gloria's family. The full names of Jean, Joy, George, and Gloria were all memorialized in the quilt that Jo made; our memories of them were stitched into the invisible fabric of our church.

Gradually, other people joined us and some mornings there were as many as thirty-five souls at the eight-thirty service in the chapel. We old-timers marvelled, counting and recounting the people in the pews to make sure we weren't dreaming.

"Thirty-five today!" someone whispered proudly to me during a service. "Including Reverend Claire, of course!" Had my mother been there, it would have been thirty-six.

Chapter Thirty-seven

Expect the Unexpected

To visit our mother's home was to be well fed.

Several years earlier, she had established a pattern, staying with us during Jamaica's hot months and fleeing back home at the first hint of cold in the fall. Much of her time was usually spent with Hamlin and me in the countryside, but after years of living with other people, Mama said she wanted to have a small place of her own.

She rented a small apartment in the city of Toronto, close to more members of the family. My brother, Michael, and sister Pat and her family all lived in the city. Although they visited us in the countryside often, Nikisha, Tim, and Lauren were living downtown, too. Lauren had gone off to university and now lived in a Toronto university dorm. Mama's new apartment made it easier for relatives and friends to visit her more often.

But no matter where Mama was, there was always good food to be had.

Her children and grandchildren were convinced that she possessed magical powers. Even seemingly empty pantries, fridges, and freezers didn't prevent her from producing a good meal, no matter what time of day you dropped in.

Even when she visited her children's homes, which was often, Mama would take control of the kitchen and, overriding our protests, prepare us a sumptuous meal.

On Mama's seventy-third birthday, she, Pat, and I were all visiting with Yvonne at her home in San Antonio, Texas. We decided that the best way to get Mama out of the kitchen was to take her to a restaurant.

A river runs right through the heart of downtown San Antonio, just steps down from street level. The famous River Walk, lined with small hotels and restaurants, wide walkways, and subtropical trees and flowers, basked in a glorious day of sunshine, blue skies, and pleasant warmth. For my two older sisters and me, this was a glorious day for a more important reason: we were all together, and Mama was alive and well and celebrating her birthday in our company.

Boatloads of tourists passed, sometimes waving at us where we sat on the restaurant patio just steps up from the water. Our mother waved back at them, laughing, her smooth light brown face radiant with joy.

At our request, Mama regaled us with stories about some of the funny moments of her life. The mood was light and at times downright hilarious: Mama's storytelling always cracked us up. Close to the end of the meal, she gave thanks to us and to God for giving her a lovely day. Gratitude was part of our mother's daily life.

"Is there anything you would like to have that you don't already?" I suddenly asked. I was thinking of something like a trip to the Holy Land or somewhere else that she had always wanted to visit, something that the children and grandchildren could pool our resources and arrange for her.

All eyes turned to our mother's face. As if she had already expected this moment to come, she answered deliberately, "To know that my children know God as well as I do."

Silence descended upon the table. No one knew what to say. Finally, my sister Pat burst out, looking at me, "Well, thanks a lot for changing the mood!"

The silence was uncomfortable only for us; our mother sat serene. She had been asked a question, and she had answered it. If we were uncomfortable, that was our business.

"If I live to be a hundred, Mama, I'm not sure I will ever know God as well as you do," I said, leaning in and touching her arm to take away the sting of my words. "You and He are practically on a first-name basis. My faith in God, meanwhile, is like Swiss cheese – all holey."

I tried to laugh. She didn't.

~

Mama's love seemed boundless, her wisdom always on tap, her funny bone always ready for a workout. She had a policy: children and grandchildren could call on her at any time of day – to share a joke, good news, a problem or even a bit of heartbreak – and know that she would laugh, take joy, commiserate with us, and pray with us. She changed her plans at the last minute if a grandchild asked to visit, or one of her children called and suggested a day outing. But it was her faith – anchored in her belief in the goodness of God, along with a certainty that things would go well – that kept us astounded.

Mama had one wish about the end of her days, that God would take her swiftly and spare her a lingering death. Having cared for her grandmother, mother, and husband in their final days, she did not want to burden her own children with her care.

"It wouldn't be a burden," we hastened to assure her.

"You have no idea what is involved in taking care of someone who is dying," she would say, lovingly but firmly. She was so adamant on this point that, as time went along,

I found myself praying for a carefully worded version of the same thing, that our mother would live for as long as she could enjoy her life and independence, and then, that her wish for a quick death would be granted.

～

It was early autumn, my favourite time of year. Mama was visiting our home – a frequent occurrence, although she still kept her small apartment in the city. Knowing that she always said her prayers after waking up, I had learned not to rush in after hearing her move around in her bedroom. I always waited for her to open her bedroom door before knocking on her door and offering her a cup of tea.

Her eyes looked tired that morning.

"I had the strangest dream," she said.

"What was it about?"

"I dreamt that we were walking along a road, when suddenly, a huge bull came charging at you. I pushed you out of the way, and stood in front of the bull. He came at me instead."

My mother fell silent.

"What a terrible dream, Mama," I said, moving quickly to hug her. "That must have been awful for you. I am so sorry."

It briefly occurred to me that she had taken the dream as an omen – Jamaicans believe that powerful dreams are not to be taken lightly – but I did not discuss it in those terms. I was not used to seeing my mother looking shaken, and all I wanted to do at the time was comfort her.

"It's just a dream, Mama; just a dream," I said.

I hugged her again, tight, willing the nightmare away. She seemed to want to say more, but stopped herself.

"Would you like your tea now?" I asked gently, finally pulling away.

She nodded, not quite meeting my eyes.

Briefly I thought of asking her, "What happened after you stepped in the way to protect me? Did you survive?" But the last thing I wanted to do was make her relive a terrible nightmare.

~

The next three weeks were unremarkable, except for one Saturday when I felt an overwhelming urge to visit my mother in her apartment. As she accepted the pot of blue and white African violets and the bag of groceries that I brought, her soft face was radiant with welcome. We sat at her small dining table, sipping our cups of tea and catching up on our week. I was about to leave when she stopped me, insisting that I eat the chicken dish she had prepared for my visit. It was, as usual, delicious.

"Think I'll ever be this good a cook?" I asked.

"Of course you will," she said. Her face and voice expressed both confidence and faith. "You are already a good cook. You just have to believe it."

"But how do you always whip up a wonderful meal out of practically nothing?" I asked, for the umpteenth time in my life.

"Little is much when God is in it," she replied, this time sending me a meaningful glance.

Time with my mother was a precious gift that always left me with a heart-filling certainty that, in that moment, all was well with the world. In recent years, I had taken to thanking her for her presence in my life. On this visit, I added two more sentences: "Thank you for your faith in our family. Thank you for your prayers on our behalf."

She smiled a glorious smile.

As I said goodbye, I did what I always did: I drew close, hugged her, and told her I loved her. And she did what she always did: she gave me her special hug, accompanied by the words, "Love you, love you, LOVE you."

~

"Expect the unexpected," Mama used to say. This saying of hers had puzzled me no end when I was small. If it was unexpected, how could you expect it?

The call came in the early afternoon. Mama had fallen and was in hospital. Whether the stroke that left her unconscious had happened before or after the fall, no one knew. Within minutes, the whole family and close friends had gathered at the hospital. Mama had not only mothered her own children; she had mothered our close friends and relatives as well.

Together, we prayed for her recovery.

Mama, the positive, powerful, prayerful presence in all our lives; Mama, the giver of unconditional love; Mama, whose faith, wisdom, and good humour had seen us through challenges big and small: Mama lay helpless on a hospital bed, and there was nothing we could do now but pray. I prayed harder than I had ever prayed for anything or anyone in my whole life.

But Mama remained in a coma.

Within days, we were all to learn a harsh truth: sometimes, the answer to a prayer is a definitive no. Mama lingered just long enough for Yvonne, our eldest sister, to arrive from Texas. Only then would Mama start her final moments.

Hugging her, my cheek on her cheek, I felt her laboured breathing as though she was climbing a long hill, one last time. There was silence, and then one more breath. And suddenly there was nothing more. Mama was gone.

Stunned, we children confessed to each other that part of us always believed she would never die, and now that she had, we didn't know what to do.

My husband's mother, Merle, guided us through the first of the farewell rituals. "Mom," as we call her, had retired from nursing, where she had helped many families confused by the unfamiliar experience of dealing with the death of a loved one. Now the need was closer to home and Mom, too, was shaken. She had lost a close confidante who was only a few years older than she. Yet she remained calm as she led us through a ritual whose origins go back through several cultures and centuries: the washing of the loved one.

Each woman and girl in the immediate family was invited to wash our mother's body as it lay on the hospital bed. Dipping a cloth into a warm bowl of water, we gently washed her face and neck, our own faces wet with tears. As we tenderly wiped her caramel-coloured thighs, legs, and feet, I remarked to our sisters that despite all the many times our mother had bathed us all, this was the first time we were bathing her. Eyes widened and heads nodded in silent agreement.

"She has such perfectly shaped legs," someone noted softly. Another gift from our mother, I suddenly realized: all her daughters and granddaughters have beautiful legs.

~

"The voice is silent," wrote Hubert van Zeller in 1963. "We had expected it would be – but that the yawns and bursts of laughter will never be repeated is almost more than we can bear ..."

The funeral was held in the same church where our daughter Nikisha and son-in-law Tim had married just two years before. The same priest, Andrew, presided. The large church was packed with relatives and friends. My mother's younger brother, Edward, one of the last to leave Jamaica back in the days when the men left for jobs in England, came to Canada for the first time. He tried to eulogize her but broke down in tears.

Nikisha, who'd been particularly close to her

grandmother, bravely read one of the lessons from the Bible and got a fair way into it before being stopped by her tears. Her uncle Michael ran up to her, handing her a handkerchief. The whole church seemed to hold its breath while she recovered.

Pat, to everyone's surprise, found the strength to speak. She had agreed to represent her siblings, on one condition: she would tell only the hair-raising stories of our childhood escapades, and Mama's reactions every time she caught us in the act or learned of our adventures later.

Laughter finally erupted in the sombre church as Pat described our perilous journeys through the culvert, the time the goats dragged us down the hill, the time she and I stole out one late evening to steal the oranges, and Mama's way of using old sayings to teach us important life lessons.

The following days were a blur of memories, sorrow, and activity. Despite my own loss, I had two daughters, sisters, a brother, a husband, cousins, uncles, and aunts – all of whom had loved Mama dearly – to support. It kept me busy, at least for a while, and I tried to return to the routines of normal life. But "normal" had suddenly changed: I had never lost my mother before; having done so now, I had no clue how to deal with it. I felt gutted and chopped off at the knees in one fell swoop.

I had not imagined that anything could hurt this badly.

An instant after I woke up each morning, the awful reality hit. The heartbreak felt like more than I could bear. I was stunned to realize that I, who had planned the transformation of teams, programs, and whole organizations, could not strategize or talk my way out of this.

Grief does not serve fair warning: all it took was a familiar sound, a sight, a smell, or a sudden memory and the pain would strike, causing me to double over, gasping.

I had been banished to the Land of Grief. I was in enemy territory without a plan, a time line, or any suitable weapons. Worse, there was no substance where my gut used to be, just a big gaping hole.

At work or in community service, I had seemed fearless to many, taking on the seemingly impossible challenges and almost always succeeding. What only I knew was that my mother had been a big part of that fierce strength. Mama was my source of unconditional love, my tower of strength, my fountain of hope and faith. In times of trouble, I always knew I could go home or call home. And always, her unshakable faith had helped reduce the problem to a manageable size.

Now, however, I was up against my biggest challenge, and it was no use calling home.

I tried to explain it to my journal: "It is the greatest of ironies: this is the most painful time of my life, the time I need my mother most. And yet I can't call home: it is my mother's death that I am mourning."

It was time to face the awful truth. No longer would my mother come to visit. No longer would I be able to call home to share a joke or a piece of good news with her. No longer would I be able to go home to the family homestead, knowing that she'd be there, arms open wide, ready with wisdom, food, and laughter, ready to counsel me about life's toughest challenges.

~

My mother's strong faith had seen her through the deaths of her grandmother, mother, and husband, but even with that faith, she had suffered through long periods of profound grief. I, the half-believer, had no such reserves to draw on.

One day, as I stood staring into the abyss, I got a bit of insight into the foundations of my own belief system: it wasn't God I had believed in. What I had trusted was my mother's faith in the being she called "Father God" when she prayed.

In times of great celebration or trouble, I had knelt beside her as she prayed, a steady calm filling my body and mind. And so I tried it now, falling to my knees and crying out to my mother's God in longer prayers than I had ever been able to muster, most starting with, "If you really are there, God …," or "I'm sorry I don't always believe in you, God …," or "If you are hearing this, God …"

Admittedly, it was not the most confident way to begin, but it was the best I could do at the time.

And just in case God was there, and heard my words, I also asked direct questions: "Why have you taken my mother?"

I pleaded for clues: "What did the bad dream mean? Was it a warning that I should have kept her close, that I should have kept a more watchful eye on her?"

And, finally, the worst question of all, the one I had never voiced but the one that sometimes sneaked up on me in the middle of the night: "Did my mother die in my place? Did she take a death that had been meant for me?"

If there was an answer, I didn't hear it. And if I heard it, I didn't understand it.

I thought that understanding my grief better would help me cut it short, manage it better, or just keep it under wraps, and went in search of books – secular books, scientific books, books on mourning and grief. They told me what I already sensed: the sudden loss of a loved one can be harder to handle than one that had been expected; the loss of a parent or a child was among the most difficult to deal with.

"Tell me something I don't know!" I yelled at these books. There was no quick cure to be had.

In the weeks after my mother's death, I had asked for

her most cherished book, her old Bible. Perhaps here I would find the comfort she had found, the faith she had developed. The Old Testament Psalms, the New Testament letters written by the apostle Paul – these had been among her favourites. Paul's writing – to the Corinthians, the Romans, the Ephesians, and others – was alternately thoughtful, beautiful, challenging. The Psalms of faith and comfort provided me with moments of respite, and for a while, I believed that God would lead me "beside still waters," that he would "restore my soul."

But sometimes, in the dead of night, the writings I read most were the Psalms of anger and lamentation, written by someone who was fed up with God's mysterious ways, someone who felt deeply disappointed in God. "My God, my God, why hast thou forsaken me?" pleaded David, psalmist and king. "Why art thou so far from helping me, from my words of groaning? … I cry by day, but thou dost not answer, and by night, but find no rest."

I didn't recognize the obvious irony in my feelings: How can you be disappointed with someone you don't believe in?

Chapter Thirty-eight

A Wish Granted

One day, months after my mother's death, I came across a slender book that was being given away at the end of a used-books sale. It was C.S. Lewis's *A Grief Observed*, his account of the days and months of his intense grief after the death of his wife, Joy.

One passage jumped out at me, so well did it capture the pain I still felt whenever I realized that Mama was gone.

"How often – will it be for always?" Lewis asked. "How often will the vast emptiness astonish me like a complete novelty and make me say: 'I never realized my loss till this moment?' "

There were times when the dark veil of grief parted just long enough to allow a moment of clarity. In my journal, I wrote the words that came in one of those moments: "If we live long enough, love deeply enough, grief is the price we pay for love. And yet, who would want to live without love? Who would want to have missed having a mother like mine?"

The call of a robin rang out from a nearby tree. Spring was finally on its way. My mother usually spent the winter months in Jamaica, returning to us in Canada in the spring. I started toward the phone to tell her what I always did at this time of year: "No more lolling about in the sunshine and hot weather down there in Jamaica! The robins have come back and so must you!"

In an instant, I was staring into the abyss. Grief wasn't done with me yet.

Then one afternoon, in the silence that followed a moment of railing at God yet again for taking our mother from us without warning, I had a sudden memory. Our mother had prayed repeatedly about the manner of her own death. She wanted it to be quick. She prayed that she would not suffer or be a burden to her children. I had understood so well how much this meant to her that even I, the unbeliever, had prayed repeatedly that she would be granted her wish.

"There are none so blind as those who will not see," my mother used to tell me, half-teasing, half-serious, on those occasions when the truth about something was staring me in the face but I was valiantly marching right past it.

Now, with a startled intake of breath, I understood: my mother's wish had been granted.

Part Five

The Old Farmhouse

When the shelter is sure,
the storm is good.

~ Henri Bosco

Chapter Thirty-nine

Mysterious Charms

It was a season of goodbyes.

Over several months, the challenge had been confronted and the decision finally made: we would have to move closer to the city.

It was a tough decision. We'd been living in paradise, surrounded by woods, streams, meadows, and flowering vines, and we knew it.

But our consulting business in the city was growing rapidly. And, as more people and cars moved into the village and surrounding areas, travel to and from the city was taking longer and longer.

And so we listed our sweet blue house in the country.

At the same time, another couple decided to move, to be closer to their daughter and her family who lived out of town. Their old farmhouse on the edge of Toronto, just a half-hour drive from our office, was up for sale.

We went to inspect the place and were immediately impressed by the land and trees surrounding it. Towering maple trees and blue-green spruce. Big old apple trees, flowering shrubs, and a sprawling lawn. It was as though we were back in the countryside.

"It has a surprising feel of privacy," said Hamlin, who, after spending almost all his career in the public spotlight of television news, yearned for peace and quiet wherever he lived.

With its welcoming verandahs, soaring mullioned windows, and thick, thick walls, this was a house designed to let the sunshine in while protecting those inside from the blowing winds and biting cold of winter.

Inside, there was a handsome maple staircase and gleaming wide-planked floors; baseboards that measured nearly eighteen inches high; tall windows and high ceilings that were framed with classic wood moulding.

On our first visit, Hamlin said the house reminded him of the farmhouse in Warkworth that his family once owned and we had tended on weekends. Then he climbed the wide maple staircase and disappeared into the house's nooks and crannies.

When he finally emerged, he said he had felt "embraced" by the house the moment he walked in. Then he beamed a smile of such joy, my heart lurched inside me. There and then, I knew it. We were goners, captivated by an old house with mysterious charms. Our eyes shone with daydreams and almost forgotten memories. Along with a thought: our family could be happy here.

There was one downside. Although the old house was set on more than a half acre of land, big, modern houses flanked it on both sides, all dating to a recent period in house building when brown brick, concrete steps, and wrought-iron railings were all the rage.

We met the owner of the old farmhouse. Tall, well spoken, apparently about eighty years old, she spoke with an upper-class English-Canadian accent. We chatted comfortably about the property.

Until we asked about the neighbours.

"I wouldn't know," she said tersely. "I don't really talk to them."

"But you mentioned that you've lived here longer than all of them," I said. "How can you avoid talking to them?"

When she answered, her gaze was steady, her tone even. All the land on which the rows of new houses now sat had once belonged to her husband and her. Their children had grown up here, ridden horses here, and roamed the acreage around the house and barns. But as the years went by, they were forced to sell pieces of the land to survive. An acre here. Another acre there. A precious old barn had been demolished. Until, finally, the old farmhouse on its less-than-one-acre lot was all that was left.

There was something else. The builders who had bought the land had broken their promise to build houses that fit in with her gracious Victorian-Georgian house. As if that wasn't enough, they had broken another promise: to make a heritage garden in the neighbourhood.

"I never got used to seeing those modern-looking houses there," she said, showing a hint of anger. She turned to look out her window. "So, other than the couple on the left and another couple who moved away, I just never bothered to get to know the neighbours. My husband talked to a few of them, but I didn't."

"You mean ... you've resented them for being here ... all these years?" I asked.

"Yes."

Hamlin asked a question that he thought was safe.

"What about the wisteria vine? Has it ever bloomed?"

She was suddenly defensive.

"Why do you ask?"

"Well, because ours is eight years old and has never bloomed. Not even once."

"Mine is fourteen years old," she said. "I've tried everything the books tell you to do, but it never bloomed. My children and husband laugh at me every spring, because I keep threatening to chop it down, but really ... I've never stopped hoping for blooms."

Misery does love company, I thought. Now we were laughing together.

Months later, we put in our offer. After some wrangling and backing-and-forthing, the old farmhouse was ours.

Chapter Forty

Terror

The months before we moved were a time of shimmering hope. That, in itself, was surprising. I had felt disloyal at the very thought of leaving the blue house, but now, having found the farmhouse, that feeling was replaced by a stronger one. We looked to the future and hoped.

As I planned our leave-taking of one home, I daydreamed about the other.

In my mind, I planned family dinners, birthday parties, even Easter egg hunts for young relatives.

In my mind, Hamlin and I created beautiful gardens that we could see through every window. We planned to build sturdy wooden arbours at each of the two gates, and I could already see climbing vines blooming in the sunshine. Red or pink roses. Clematis vines in blue or pink. Or purple. Honeysuckle vines? Yes, perhaps. The kind that has creamy yellow blooms that smell like lemon. And places to sit and enjoy the garden, of course. We would place one bench here, another one over there, right under that tree.

In my mind, I saw a home of warmth and happy times. As I stood in the kitchen of our blue house, wrapping dishes and packing them into boxes, I looked ahead to my favourite holiday season, Christmas. I saw my family decorating the house with evergreen wreaths, golden angels, and beeswax candles, the presents under the Christmas tree, every room bathed in the warm glow of this sacred and happy time.

Through the tall mullioned windows, I saw the branches of the elegant blue-green spruce trees at the far end of the back lawn of our new home. Except now they were strung with tiny white lights that shone through the branches like fairy lights, sprinkling the darkness with magic.

We would be happy there. I knew it. And knowing it made my heart sing a little, even as we planned our departure from the house and grounds we loved so much.

I felt one tremor of trepidation, but only one. As if to remind myself of our family's good fortune, I drove by the farmhouse one afternoon. I slowed right down, looked up at it – at this tall, even grand two-storey red-brick building – and stopped. A strange thought pierced my mind.

Would the people who built this house, the people who had lived here in the 1860s, approve of us? For that matter, would the house itself approve of us?

Something about this house made me question my right to live here, as though I wasn't good enough and the house already knew it.

It wasn't the price. In fact, because of its location outside the city, this house cost roughly the same as a small dwelling in downtown Toronto. The farmhouse wasn't even the biggest house on the street, although, because it was set on a slight incline, and had high ceilings on both floors, its roofline towered over all the others.

Perhaps that was it: the soaring roofline. Or the massive trees and wooden fence, which allowed glimpses of the house's solid red brick façade but protected it from being fully scrutinized by peering eyes. Whatever it was, the house suddenly appeared aloof, even forbidding.

Were my family and I overreaching? Or, as Jamaicans would say, were our eyes bigger than our stomachs? By wanting to live in this house, after nearly a decade in a humble little house in the woods, were we pretending to be more than we were?

And then, about as quickly as they had entered my mind, the thoughts disappeared, and my body relaxed immediately. I had lived in bigger houses than this, I thought, houses with a lot more acreage. I chided myself for being silly.

~

Arriving back at the blue house, I consulted my carefully drawn-up lists and continued preparing for the move. The packing, the address changes, the calls about disconnection and connection dates for telephone, electricity, and cable. It was a whirlwind, but one that had been carefully designed and was going according to plan. I had everything under control.

And then.

Exactly two weeks before moving day, on a glorious, almost-summer day in late June, another car crashed into the back of mine.

There were witnesses to the collision, but I remembered little. A feeling of sudden terror. A policeman's face, saying words I couldn't quite hear. I remembered trying to put my glasses back on my face. Nothing else.

Over the following days, instead of hurrying around packing the final items for the move, I was in medical clinics, doctors' offices, and finally back in my own bed, struggling to believe what had happened.

It was a bewildering time, made worse by pain, worry, and recurring flashbacks to the accident. Unable to sleep without having nightmares, unable to ride in a car without involuntary screaming, I soon became aware of how much control I had lost. Unable to eat proper meals because of cracked teeth, hounded by fears about my damaged eye and the realization that my lower right side, left shoulder, and neck appeared to be getting worse, not better ... I was a boiling cauldron of worries.

On moving day, the pain that possessed my body seemed to have gone ahead of me into the new house, painting every room a shade of desperation.

Meanwhile, small things – taking a bath, brushing my teeth – required massive amounts of effort. I had to manoeuvre the toothbrush and water carefully around the cracks in my teeth, because if the water seeped through, it would trigger sharp pain from exposed nerves. Changing my clothes, or styling my hair – these were exercises in futility.

Days became weeks, then months. Our daughters did their best to help, while coping with their own lives. Most days, it was Hamlin who combed my hair, helped me dress, helped me walk, while now shouldering the entire burden of our growing business.

Every plan we had made was predicated on my helping to run our company and our home. And now, despite occasional bursts of determined effort to go to work, I couldn't sit, stand, or think for long periods. Speaking fluently – finding the words, holding a thought, things that I'd taken for granted – that was now a lost skill.

I returned to bed. Time marched on without me.

Every room in the house now seemed grey and dreary, except for the carpet in the living room and hallways. Earlier, its patterns of swirling red, gold, and brown had seemed warmly autumnal; now they resembled the tongues of angry flames. I imagined this carpet covering the floor in one of Dante's circles of hell.

For a few days, I even became convinced that the old blue and white wallpaper in our bedroom – which I had found charming when I first saw it – contained unfriendly ghosts. On days when I was alone in the house, I even yelled at them from time to time, daring them to show their faces.

Chapter Forty-one

Hamlin Plants Flowers

I worried most about Hamlin.

He was the family member who had taken the brunt of the fallout from the accident, but no one was tending to him. I had always known him to be courageous, but his courage was tested by this crisis over and over.

In the first three years after the accident, I'd been seen by umpteen doctors and therapists, undergone dozens of tests and assessments, and been prescribed a battery of medications and injections for pain, anxiety, and insomnia.

I had physiotherapy of various kinds, bought an astonishing number of very ugly shoes and boots to accommodate my injured foot, been introduced to an even uglier variety of leg braces, and purchased every kind of pain relief system that Hamlin and I had heard about, from Asian ointments to prescription drugs to electronic pain busters.

Our bed became the site of daily battles with pain, our bedroom a battlefield littered with discarded weapons. On my dresser stood small plastic jars of prescription pills, lined up like soldiers who had forgotten their purpose. On the floor at my bedside like an altar to failure was an untidy pile of contraptions: expensive, strange-looking objects, bought to zap the pain away.

We were spending tens of thousands of dollars to help me get better so I could return to work, to life. But there were no contraptions to help my husband, no doctors pondering over his injuries, no medications or programs prescribed for what he was going through. Yet this man had lost so much. His business partner. His active wife who took joy in life, who used to tease him when he got too serious. His friend, his lover, his dance partner. His partner on long walks in the country. His very independence. He had lost it all.

Once in a while, I worried that he'd even lose himself.

Hamlin got through the days, sometimes barely. On top of running the business, paying the bills, cooking, and transporting me around, he had to wash my back, help me dress, even comb my unruly hair.

We still shared a bed, but badly. My half of the bed was filled with pillows of various shapes and sizes, used to prop me up and hold me in that precise angle where my left shoulder, right side, neck, back, and leg were protected enough to allow me to fall asleep. Some nights, it took two hours to negotiate a truce between the bed, the pillows, and my inflamed body parts. Most nights, there was no truce.

If I fell asleep, there was worse to come. The moment I turned in my sleep, a sharp, hot knife slashed through my shoulder, neck, or back, and without knowing it, I screamed.

And it got even worse. If I was able to enter a dream state, the nightmares began: over and over, I watched my loved ones dying in fatal accidents while I looked on, unable to help. Each time, my screams filled the bedroom for long seconds.

In my zombie state, it didn't even occur to me to sleep in the guest room and if it occurred to Hamlin, he didn't say. Instead, he was fighting back. He was refusing to give up, and doing so in unusual ways. One of his biggest strategies involved the garden.

~

Two months before we moved into the old farmhouse, we had received the owners' permission to create a few garden beds near the front verandah and begin transferring plants to them.

Hamlin and I divided up our favourite plants and put them in large plastic pots for the journey. We even separated a small sucker from the non-blooming wisteria vine.

"I figure it's got about as much chance at blooming as the parent plant," Hamlin said, shaking his head at our inability to get our wisteria vine to bloom.

Some of the pots contained flowering perennials that Marion and Henry had given us several years earlier. Other pots were gifts from friends Les and Sandra.

"Glad to hear you're getting a head start on the new garden," Sandra said. "I can't imagine you two moving to a place that has no garden."

"We'll have to bring you some more plants," said Les. "How about some more hosta? And other stuff, of course."

And so it was that we received an abundance of plants from friends. Hosta, Solomon's seal, pink flowering anemones, and a fern-leaf peony from Les and Sandra; daylilies and a large pink bleeding heart peony from Jean and Bill; and red poppies and plants without names from Gundy and Peter.

It was just as well. By the time we moved in, that summer, I was unable to do any gardening at all, and Hamlin was suddenly faced with new priorities.

Back in the time of daydreams, back in those exciting months before we moved into the farmhouse, I had planned to have a garden arbour or two, supports for the clematis vines I planned to plant in certain places in the garden. I had given up on that by now.

But Hamlin hadn't. First, he built me one garden arbour, then another. Day after day he was in the garden, silently cutting and staining the wood, hammering nails, creating latticework on the tops and sides of the arbours to support the vines in their upward climb. One arbour stood right in the centre of the back garden. I could see the clematis vines climb up it, their large round pink and purple blooms open to the sun, on those summer days when I sat on the verandah, and even on days when I was stuck upstairs in bed.

I remembered our first garden and how Hamlin had insisted that the only thing worth growing was something we could eat. But now he was trying his best to get through to me, and he was doing it in a variety of ways. Building me garden arbours and planting flowering vines were two of those ways.

The third was to tell me how much he relied on me.

""Even in this state, even when you're flying on one wing – or no wing at all – you are my strength," he said. "You have to believe that."

I needed to believe that. With the results of the various medical assessments done and redone, I was facing an inescapable truth: my injuries weren't just physical. The accident had left me with a head injury and two more unpleasant outcomes: post-traumatic stress and severe depression.

These were the scary things that had lurked in the shadows of my mind. Now they had been given names.

Some people have an accident and end up with a broken leg. I had ended up with a broken life.

Unable to talk about the enormity of these things with other human beings, I returned to talking to the house, and sometimes to God. In my mind.

Chapter Forty-two

Homecoming Days

In the days after we'd first visited the house, I had tried to imagine the farmhouse a hundred and forty years earlier when it was built. Back then it would have been surrounded by hundreds of acres of fields, trees, and streams.

The house was roughly the same age as Canada. The farmhouse was completed in two parts: in 1865 and 1870. Canadian Confederation, the coming together of Canada's regions to form one country, took place in 1867. It must have been a time of great hope.

After our offer to buy was accepted, I went looking for information about the house's early history, but little was known about the first family who had lived here. They were known to have come to Canada from Scotland. But unlike some other pioneer families, they didn't leave behind any letters or journals chronicling their lives.

Maybe, I thought back then, one of the families who had lived here would show up after we moved in and tell us what they knew.

Now, as I lay in my bed, nursing my wounds, I found myself praying that all visitors would stay away. I rarely answered the doorbell. It simply wasn't worth the effort of getting out of bed or trying to talk.

I was trapped inside a beautiful old house. Late some nights, as the pain intensified and I could hardly even breathe without suffering, I couldn't see the point in living.

This I told the old house, afraid to tell anyone else.

But the house had other ideas. It started to summon its children home.

~

The first visitor approached our front door tentatively, afraid to knock, and yet afraid not to. Afraid that we'd turn him away, and afraid that we'd let him in. After all, if everything inside had changed, would his precious memories be tarnished, even ruined?

In the end, he timidly knocked on the old farmhouse door.

When we opened the door, he stood like a deer caught in the headlights.

"This is my house!" the elderly man finally blurted out, then apologized for what he thought was a rude beginning.

We burst out laughing and welcomed him inside.

One by one and two by two, people who had lived here started to return. Asked what had made them visit decades after leaving, none of them had a logical explanation. Some said they felt inexplicably drawn to return. One man said he was "just in the neighbourhood" and thought he'd revisit "the old house." He hadn't done so since he had left five decades before.

Stranger things happened once they entered the house. It was as though, by crossing the threshold, they became children again.

Children of this house.

They walked through the rooms, caressed the walls with fingers that seemed to talk to the house, gazed out the windows as though seeing their past on our lawns.

The visitors recalled loved ones long dead, a world long gone. Their memories burst out in gales of laughter, or emerged slowly with a sense of wonder, or with tears.

They would go outside, point at the spot where a beloved horse was buried, the place where one of two wells once stood, the part of the lawn where a huge tree had fallen and provided a place for them to rest.

Sitting in our kitchen or on the verandah, they resurrected memories that had lain dormant for so long that they were surprised at what they remembered. One of them even came up with the name of the two ancient apple trees standing in our garden. Owner after owner had tried to determine their provenance. But no one had ever been able to do so. And then, on a sunny day in the springtime, Bert knocked at the door. A tall, handsome, white-haired man, now in his eighties, the one who had said, "This is my house!"

Bert had lived here as a child. It was his grandparents and parents who had built the house. He had never forgotten the apple trees, simply because he had never seen any others that bore so profusely, with apples as big as grapefruits.

"They're Wolf River apples," he told us.

"How on earth do you remember that?" Hamlin asked. "You left here more than seventy years ago."

"I have never forgotten those trees," Bert replied, "but I can't believe that I remembered the name."

A quick search on the Internet proved that Bert's memory was airtight. We learned that the apples got their name from Wolf River, Wisconsin, where a seedling was discovered in 1875. Every description fit our apples: dull-red colouring, splashed with pale pink or pale yellow patches; a single apple weighing as much as a pound or even more.

For me, each visit was a precious gift. By barging into

my life, the visitors forced me out of my bed and out of my shell, forced me to rise above my misery and take an interest in other people and their stories.

One man recalled his pride at being accepted into the riding school that was housed here in the sixties. He was the first Jewish child to do so, and he remained friends with many of the other riders over the years.

Another visitor, another story, a different emotion: one man who lived here recalled episodes of verbal and physical abuse from a member of his extended family who never fully accepted him.

"He looked at me and saw ..." He stopped, swallowed hard, and started again. "He treated me as ... not family, not even human. How can you hate a child?"

I wanted to reach into the past and comfort the child. And while there, I wanted to confront the adult who hurt this child, this precious child who now sat in front of me, still wounded by those cruel blows of long ago.

But it was too late. The harm had been done.

I sat down at the harvest table in my kitchen, crying alongside my visitor. Then he glimpsed a happy memory and got up and walked through the house, touching the walls, talking to the house. He even seemed to listen for a reply.

Only one other visitor had ever done this: Bert. He returned to visit us every spring, a bit frailer each time, yet determined to walk through the house and outside to the apple trees, as though making a sacred pilgrimage. On his latest visit, he and I propped each other up with an arm around each other's waist.

As Bert touched the trees, the walls, the doors, looking around at the scenes of his childhood, I was never sure what his reaction would be: sorrow or joy. Sometimes he wept softly; other times he laughed; sometimes he ended up doing both.

"My mother used to have tea parties," he said. "She'd dress up my brother and me in our best clothes and tell us how to behave like real hosts. We'd stand at the door in our long pants and long-sleeved shirts to welcome the ladies to the house and take their coats.

"Oh, dear, oh, dear," he said, still smiling at the memory while reaching for his handkerchief to wipe his eyes. "I loved those times."

One evening, he phoned me.

"Cynthia!" he said. "You know, there's a very important thing I keep meaning to tell you. But then I start talking about the past and I completely forget, every time."

"What is it, Bert?"

"I keep wanting to tell you that if my parents and grandparents were here, they would love you."

I was speechless. Finally, I blurted, "Shocked, you mean! Shocked to see these Jamaican people living in the nice house they built for their family!"

I was laughing now, teasing Bert in the easy way that had developed between us.

"Cynthia," Bert said. "I'm serious. You and your family – you're special people, you know. If my parents and grandparents were here, they'd thank you and Hamlin for taking such good care of our house ..."

He paused and I waited silently.

"... and for welcoming my daughter and me to visit ... and for being such good people. They would thank you. And since they're not here to do it, I want to thank you."

A lump formed in my throat.

"Thank you, Bert," I croaked.

Chapter Forty-three

A Thing of Beauty

The visitors and their stories were a tonic to my battered soul. Now the house and I had finally been properly introduced to each other, after all those nights in which, unable to sleep or find comfort, I had stayed awake talking to it. The house was finally talking back. Through its children.

The old house itself needed some loving care. Hamlin and I could see it in the timeworn carpets and kitchen cabinets that needed to be replaced, the verandah posts that needed repairs. But the house spoke to us unequivocally when its cast iron pipes that ran through the bathrooms burst. Not only the plumbing, but also the ceiling of the room below – the kitchen – needed repair.

The upstairs bathrooms and kitchen below them were situated in the older part of the house. Despite the emergency, Hamlin and I were eager to see what lay between the upstairs floors and the kitchen ceiling.

The plumber was impressed by the cast iron drainpipes that ran from bathrooms and kitchen and down to the sewer below.

"Look at this!" he said. "With cast iron this thick, you don't hear a thing, no matter how many times you flush the toilets or take a bath!"

We already knew this to be true but went to look anyway.

Craftsmen who came to repair the ceiling looked at its innards, impressed by how well the farmhouse had been built more than a century before.

"Look at those joists!" one carpenter called out to the other workers. "You don't see this kind of thing anymore."

Indeed, the big wooden joists that held the floor up, above the kitchen, were perfect. They were exactly the same width, height, and distance apart from one another. One man took out his tape measure and confirmed the measurements.

"Remarkable, amazing," he said. He shook his head while searching for more superlatives. "A thing of beauty."

The poet-carpenter and other craftsmen walked through the house, admiring its parts and declaring that every window – and the framing around it – was a treasure. Every baseboard and door, every built-in cupboard, every bit of paneling in the library, the dining room, or the hallway – everything was made from very thick wood and was a thing of rare beauty.

Indeed, the tall staircase, the herringbone-patterned wood floors in the dining room, the wide-planked floors in the bedrooms, even the doorknobs spoke of another time. They also spoke of the care that family after family had shown.

"Think we can make money from giving carpenters tours of our old house?" I asked Hamlin.

The work completed, the bills paid, the workmen said goodbye. We walked through the house, admiring it by ourselves, seeing it with new eyes. Hamlin had never stopped loving this house. One look and he had fallen in love. But I had arrived here injured and angry and had lost my enthusiasm for it.

Now I was finally starting to love the house. Again.

Chapter Forty-four

Setback

I should have known it was too good to last.

After all, when had my relationship with my homes been predictable? For that matter, when had my own life ever been predictable?

One day, my leg collapsed. This was not surprising; my back, leg, and foot had been damaged in the accident, and I fell often. But this time I was at the top of the stairs, had taken my first step, and went flying.

Trying to stop the fall, I slammed my left foot against the railing, which caused my head to slam into the wall opposite. Just as my head made contact, I remembered that even the interior walls of this house were made of brick or stone.

When I opened my eyes, I was at the foot of the stairs and Hamlin was bending over me, shocked. I could barely see him. Instead, I saw a big dark blob, edged with what seemed like a shade of lavender. When Hamlin tried to help me up, everything hurt, but I was so dazed, I didn't know how bad the damage was.

~

I tried to describe it in my diary in the following months.

Now both feet are damaged and I can't walk at all. Two front teeth are chipped. As if all that weren't bad enough, my good eye – my right eye – is blurry.

I'm confined to bed, swallowing painkillers day and night. The zombie-like state has returned. I can barely speak. Everything is grey and depressing.

I'm trapped inside this house all over again.

~

Hamlin sat beside me on the bed and talked to me softly. I noticed, really noticed, that much of his hair had fallen out and what was left had turned grey. He looked the way I felt: worried, tired, defeated. It was in his hair and eyes, the lines in his face, the droop of his shoulders.

"I'm the cause of all this," I told myself. I stared at my husband through the haze that stood between me and everyone else. "I have ruined this good man's life."

~

Some people possess a radar, a kind of homing instinct, that tells them it's time to come home. Lauren is one such person.

Perceptive in the extreme, she spots things that no one else sees. You might tell her that nothing is wrong, but she sees the truth behind your claim.

Hamlin and I had agreed that we didn't want our children to worry about me; we wanted them to focus on school and work.

Truth is, I didn't want them to see how bad my condition was some days, especially now, after the fall down the stairs. Nikisha and Tim were both in very demanding careers that required them to travel. I was relieved that they couldn't visit often.

Lauren, too, had a hectic schedule in the early years after the accident. She was away at school and also had a busy part-time job.

"Don't you want me to come home this weekend and help out?" she phoned to ask.

"You have a lot on your shoulders right now," we always assured her. "Focus on school and work."

But, sensing that something was wrong, Lauren started coming home. Not asking, just coming home.

It didn't take her long to see that I was not as well as I pretended. That I spent entirely too much time in bed. That my left arm still didn't work, that my right leg still tended to collapse, that my left foot was a bizarre shade of purple and black from the fall down the stairs. That walking was painful, getting up from a chair was a major production, and that I never tried to climb the stairs when anyone could see me. That when I talked, I often made no sense at all.

Lauren watched me out of the corner of her eye, worrying.

I begged her not to.

Now I understood how my mother felt when she told us that she wanted a quick death. That she didn't want to get ill and linger, becoming a burden to her children.

Lauren finally returned to school, still worrying.

She had a right to worry. I was falling. Not on the street, not down the stairs, but out of everything.

I no longer felt at home in this world. Not in this house, not with my family, not in my bed, not even in my own skin. I still wrote in my journal, but entry after entry reeked of desperation.

A life this painful is not worth living, I thought.

And then a visitor arrived.

Damn, damn, damn.

I was in a deep dark hole, lacking the strength to make the long climb back out. I didn't want to see anyone, talk to anyone, smile with anyone. But my husband welcomed the man to come inside and meet with me.

In the course of talking about his life in the old house, the visitor started to tell me a story. Then, noticing the strange look on my face, he stopped, afraid to say more. Surprising myself, I pressed him to continue.

Some decades earlier, he explained, his ancestor who owned the farm had a stroke and became unable to tend the land or the animals. The stroke also damaged his speech. Unwilling to accept a life of greatly reduced mobility and a new dependence on others, the farmer fell into a deep depression. He lay in bed, rousing himself occasionally only to eat or sit in his favourite chair. Even going outside to look at his fields and dairy herd upset him, so he rarely did so.

Everyone – his wife, children, and other relatives – thought he'd snap out of his dark mood eventually. Instead, one night while everyone slept, the farmer took his shotgun, walked to the barn farthest from the house, and killed himself.

No one had even known that he could walk that far.

As I listened to the visitor, I followed the farmer as he struggled to walk the distance to the barn farthest from the house. I knew that he made the slow, extremely painful journey because he didn't want to taint the family home with his brutal death. That he wanted to get as far away from it as possible to do this necessary deed.

I understood the despair that drove him to end his own life.

For weeks now, I had been able to focus on only one thing: my own death.

Suddenly, I felt frightened. Hours later, sobbing, I told my husband that I had fallen into a deep pit and couldn't climb my way out.

Chapter Forty-five

Crying Over Red Shoes

How could I explain?

How could I explain the awful thoughts that went through my mind late at night when pain kept me awake while everyone else was asleep? The nights when I talked to a house, listened for an answer, and then got angry because the house did not reply?

How could I explain to anyone sane that, while trying to cheer myself up by leafing through a glossy magazine one day, I saw a picture of a pair of shiny red high-heeled shoes – the kind of shoes I will never be able to wear again because of my injured foot, leg, and back – and bawled furiously for at least two minutes?

A grown woman crying over red shoes? How ridiculous can you get?

But, worst of all, how to explain my constant worry that we'd lose our house, the house my husband loved? Hamlin was determined to hold on to it, but with so many expenses and only one income over several years, we very well could lose it unless I could start earning an income again.

It was now autumn. My doctor had enrolled me at the rehabilitation hospital, in a special program for people with chronic pain who wanted to find new ways of managing it without relying on drugs. Much of the program was carried out by therapists working with small groups.

We patients learned a variety of techniques. Techniques to manage the pain, renegotiate our primary relationships, and even to continue living in the homes we loved and didn't want to leave.

This program, however, was so demanding that it made returning to narcotic painkillers a very attractive option. With a head injury, severe pain, and not enough sleep, I found myself constantly flailing in the workshops – and in the hot-water therapy pool.

~

"Now we're going to move both our arms and legs together," the physiotherapist announced. "Like this!"

She demonstrated, then glanced in my direction.

"Cynthia!" she called out. "You ..." She was about to correct me for the umpteenth time, but smiled instead. "You just do whatever it is that you're doing."

Over and over, I did the one thing that I could always manage: marching-hopping-staggering on the spot. For months I marched, my concentration so intense that I barely noticed anyone else. But it wasn't enough.

Sometimes I'd try so hard, so furiously, to move my injured limbs that I'd gasp, my face crumpled and wet with tears from pain. But I kept going. Until a watchful therapist would holler: "No more, Cynthia! Stop right now!"

One day, after a fierce effort, I blacked out from excruciating pain, in the deep end of the pool. A woman and two men nearby moved in swiftly to help. But lead therapist Lynette was not nearly so accommodating.

"We can't have you doing this, Cynthia."

Her alarm made her British accent particularly pronounced.

"If you continue to put yourself at risk, we will have to ask you to leave."

Chapter Forty-six

Words Fail Me

Words had been essential to my life for as long as I could remember.

Words of comfort, shared with my husband, children, parents, sisters, brother, and other loved ones.

Words of encouragement, argument, agreement. Words of gratitude, words of love.

Words. I had learned to love them when I was just a small child. And when I'd started high school at such a young age, my love of words helped me survive in a land of giants. I had read books in several languages, some of which I'd taught myself. I had debated with the headmaster, then in front of the whole school.

I had gone on to make an excellent living with the help of words. Words read, words written, words listened to; words spoken in guidance, praise, criticism, question, or debate; words spoken in different languages. Words spoken on television, in executive boardrooms, in keynote presentations across the globe.

Words had helped me build a career, win award after award, each more prestigious than the one before.

My confidence with words had also helped give me an international profile. I had co-led the Canadian team that helped transform the South African Broadcasting Corporation at the end of apartheid. I became secretary general for the international public television board called INPUT, based in Canada and Italy. Being able to speak English, French, Spanish, and some Italian made me comfortable on the world stage.

And when I had started a company with my husband – one that thrived in its consulting work with a variety of companies across Canada and in Europe – adapting words to different environments had proven an essential skill.

Nor did it stop there. I must have had a sign posted on my forehead that said, "This woman loves words." Wherever I travelled, strangers targeted me for conversation. On trains and airplanes. Doctors, lawyers, businessmen. They told me words they couldn't tell their friends, wives, co-workers. And, having shared their secrets with me, they proceeded to seek my words of advice.

Eventually I had found a weapon to discourage these sudden bouts of intimacy: opening a book and making a show of peering at it right after the person seated beside me, on a long flight between home and Europe, Asia, or Africa, said hello.

But even this was an unreliable defence. For example, on a flight home from Europe, a Newfoundland businessman, seated across an empty seat to my left, simply ignored my sudden display of intense interest in my book.

"Are you married?" he asked.

"*Yes!*" I almost shouted at him, intending to shut him down.

"Well," said he, with a flirtatious smile, "do you fool around?"

In the midst of assuming a most fearsome look, I found myself laughing and settled in for what turned out to be an interesting talk.

"Conversations 'R' Us," I thought later, as I drifted off to sleep.

~

Now I had lost my words. Sometimes the words were like butterflies, flitting into my brain, but – before my tongue could articulate them – flying away again. If only there was a butterfly net to capture words.

To make matters worse, I often stuttered when I tried to speak, especially when asked about the accident or my injuries. There was a medical reason for this, but my mind couldn't grapple with the meaning of the strange words that described it.

Now my words – my friends since childhood, my friends throughout my life – were punishing me. They had made up their minds to stay away until I was willing to face those strange new *painful* words. But I could not face them just then.

Occasionally, my words would come back for a while, and I would chatter endlessly to Hamlin, afraid that if I didn't use the words, they would disappear again. Which, of course, they often did.

I adapted, sort of. If someone insisted on communicating with me, I sent an e-mail. One that would have taken a few minutes pre-accident now took an hour or more, but that was preferable to trying to talk.

I had fallen mute. As the months crawled by, I even became used to it. After all, I rarely went out. My conversations were in my own head, the words I spoke now were silent ones, addressed to my dog, my journal, my house, and God, none of which used words to talk back.

~

"What is the difference between a reaction and a response?" asked the therapist. She was leading the seminar on managing anger.

A very big man, a member of my group at the rehabilitation hospital, didn't miss a beat.

"Jail time," he said.

It cracked us up. Even I, the silent one, burst out laughing.

After months of watching them from a distance, months of saying very little to anyone, I finally started to open my eyes to those around me. One day I even caught myself thinking, "What an interesting group of people."

There were usually about twelve in the group, women and men of various ages, sizes, ethnicity, and professions. Most were highly intelligent, accomplished individuals: corporate executives, artists, academics, computer analysts, medical professionals, construction workers. One was a housewife, another a university student. Some were long retired from their careers.

They were also survivors of accidents, survivors of cancer, and, in the case of one beautiful young mother, the survivor of a botched operation.

Some of them were afflicted by something called fibromyalgia, a disease that causes pain in all the joints of the body.

As they spoke, I realized that many, like me, had dutifully taken the medications they had been prescribed until they had finally become worried about their lack of progress or about becoming dependent on drugs. So, with their doctors' support, they had started looking for new ways to fight back against the pain, to regain control of body and mind. Indeed, of their very lives.

Those who had joined the group earlier showed a special kindness toward newcomers, especially ones such as I who were still shell-shocked, dazed, or too angry to speak.

An elderly woman with short grey hair and a petite figure came over to me one day during a break and hugged me tenderly.

"Rome wasn't built in a day," she said with a knowing smile.

She was a charming woman who had just told the group about her great love of dancing and how a back injury had changed her life. She, too, had struggled with anger.

Another patient, sensing my frustration, smiled gently and told me to give myself a break. I looked her in the eye and said nothing.

"It takes time," she said, looking back at me intently. "Trust me, I know. I have chronic pain, I have a head injury, and much more. I think I know how you're feeling. It's a lot to handle all at once, isn't it? But you just have to give yourself time. Promise?"

I nodded a promise, but I didn't know if I had time. What would happen if we had to give up the home my husband loved? That would be the final straw. The very thought made me angry all over again.

The accident not only changed my life, but also damaged every aspect of it. I, the award-winning television producer, the writer, the project leader, the public speaker, the world traveller, the taker-on of impossible challenges. I, the wife, the mother, the community volunteer. I, who used to see each obstacle as a challenge, was ill prepared to deal with total failure.

Nine months after she met me, therapist Lynette confessed, "I have never come across anyone as angry as you, Cynthia. You're the angriest patient I have ever met in this program."

That made me furious, and I wanted to fight back – until I realized that I'd only be proving her right.

Later, a therapist told me that I was on a trajectory, working my way through anger and denial.

"Eventually you'll get to acceptance," she said. "It just takes time."

"Acceptance?" I threw the word back. "Sounds like giving up."

"No! Acceptance is not giving up. It's an acceptance of things the way they are, but not giving up. Meditation will help," she said. "It helps you to be mindful, to live in the moment. And to accept."

Living in the moment – being mindful of it, accepting of it, instead of worrying about what the future holds – was not easy. But I was determined to try.

~

At home, I did the breathing, meditation, and mindfulness exercises every day.

"I must accept that there are some things I can no longer do," I told myself often.

Gardening was undoubtedly one of them. It had been a favourite way for me to unwind. My fingers, my hands, my whole body loved the feel of the dirt, of moving plants around till they found their perfect places. Ever since moving into the first home Hamlin and I owned, I had loved to hide tulip and daffodil bulbs deep in the soil each autumn, looking forward to the miraculous birth each spring of what my own hands had planted.

Now I told myself that *not* gardening was one of the things I had to learn to accept. So, gripping my cane for support, I walked around my garden one late summer afternoon and told myself serenely, "It doesn't matter that the flowerbeds have become a jungle."

And then, as I surveyed the damage: "It doesn't matter that big plants seem to have literally swallowed up the smaller ones. This is just nature being nature ... a demonstration of 'survival of the biggest.' I must accept. I will accept."

And then.

I spied a big, awful, prickly, grey-green weed standing

– *flourishing* – right in the middle of my flowerbed. The healthiest, biggest bloody plant in the whole darned place.

I wanted to scream. Taking a deep breath instead, I reached down inside myself, searching for acceptance. What surfaced instead was a very bad cuss word, which I silently hurled at the monster weed.

The weed appeared to smirk.

My new-found serenity had definitely taken off and left me. I swore again. Out loud this time.

~

Hamlin took me to see a movie. It was about a powerful person who struggled to do the one thing most people take for granted: speaking without stuttering. The problem was that the man was the king of England, and as Britain headed into the Second World War, people looked to him to build morale through public speeches. The film, *The King's Speech*, moved me to tears. When the king finally managed to make his speech, I was the first person in the cinema to applaud – wildly.

~

It was in a book – a murder mystery, of all places – that I came face to face with what frightened me most: post-traumatic stress disorder. I had heard these words from doctors and therapists, but at the time, I'd had all the bad news I could handle. I had refused to say the words, vainly trying to make the diagnosis go away.

Now, in the middle of a Minette Walters novel, there it was, the frightening list of symptoms: flashbacks to the accident, nightmares, insomnia, social withdrawal, loss of appetite, profound anxiety, inability to recall the accident, thoughts of death.

I knew them all, intimately. I had lived with them since the early days after the accident. But I had never seen them listed in one place. Now I was face to face with the truth. I did, indeed, have all the symptoms of post-traumatic stress, and, added to the chronic pain, reduced mobility, and severe depression, this was a very dangerous thing to have.

"God speaks to us in mysterious ways," my mother used to say when something inexplicable had happened, something too bizarre to be simple coincidence.

My family doctor sent me to yet another therapist, one experienced in dealing with all of the above.

"I don't w-w-want to ... w-w-waste your time ... or mine," I said, when it was my turn to speak.

After a long, tortuous pause, I continued. "I know that something is very wrong with me ... I know that something has to change. But if these sessions are about talk for talk's sake, I won't come back."

"I understand," she replied. "Is there anything else you'd like to tell me?"

"Yes. That old therapist trick of saying something, then falling silent, expecting me to fill the void – it doesn't work on me. I have great difficulty speaking about these things ... and I'm now very used to silence. So we'll just sit here and stare at each other."

I spoke from notes, and it was the longest and most difficult speech I had made in a long time. But my new therapist was unfazed.

"I can work with that," she said.

It was a start.

"OK, then," I said. "Could we start with a meditation?"

Not only did we start with a meditation; we also ended every session with one. It was a necessity. At the end of that first session, I was drowning in tears, gasping for breath, and sinking fast. I was a child again, pulled down into the heavy water of the dark culvert, except that now there was no daylight on the other side, and no one could save me.

My new therapist moved in quickly. She led me through a breathing exercise, and we meditated for several minutes. For many sessions after, this was the pattern. Every session was frightening, but I kept going. After a while, I even remembered the therapist's name: Sarah.

Chapter Forty-seven

Blessings

Trust E. B. White to say it just right: "A really companionable and indispensable dog is an accident of nature. You can't get it by breeding for it and you can't buy it with money. It just happens along."

Our dog Kinu was an Akita, a breed originally from Japan. Despite his huge brown head, gigantic paws, and massive body encased in golden fur, he had a delightfully gentle nature.

But Kinu was also persistent. Most mornings during the first few years after the accident found me in bed, unwilling to incur the pain of getting up, or simply too exhausted to move. Kinu always climbed the stairs to my bedroom and nuzzled my head.

Eventually he flopped his huge frame down by my bedside and lay there for hours, snoozing, occasionally cocking his head at me as if to ask: "When on earth are you going to get up from this bed?"

One morning, Hamlin had to leave the house early because of an emergency at the office. That left Kinu with no one to take him for his walk.

"Don't worry," I said. "I'll take him."

"You sure?" Hamlin asked, staring at me in surprise.

"I'm sure," I said, feeling not at all sure. This would be my first dog walk since the accident, and I didn't know how to walk a dog and use a cane at the same time.

It took me forever to get dressed, negotiate the stairs, and join Kinu in the garden.

Normally, Kinu would romp around, tugging on his leash, impatient to get going. But this morning he did a peculiar thing. He waited patiently as I took each painful step, padding along beside me like a guide dog.

We slowly made our way around the corner and down the street. When a man approached, Kinu, ever friendly, wagged his curly tail in delight. The man asked about my injuries. I opened my mouth to speak but immediately burst into tears. I limped away, embarrassed.

After that, I kept to a pattern. Head down. No meeting anyone's eyes. If someone said "good morning" I'd say "good morning" back but keep moving – anything to avoid bursting into tears in public again.

Kinu and I had become polar opposites. I was a silent recluse, unwilling to engage with the neighbours and, on some days, with life itself. But he was everybody's friend. A four-year-old boy, less than half the size of Kinu, ran across the street, patted the dog's massive head, and announced in awe: "He smiled at me! The dog smiled at me! He's a re-ally nice dog!"

I returned to bed, exhausted.

Then, on one of my worst mornings, when my body was bent with unending pain and my mind blank with lack of sleep – a neighbour stopped us as we returned home. The man spoke to Kinu, instead of me: "How are you this morning, my friend?"

Kinu wagged his tail, sat down, and settled in for a visit. *Traitor!*

Realizing I was stuck, I forced myself to ask the man,

"And how are you?" But I didn't meet his eyes and didn't care if he answered.

"I'm a blessed man," he said softly. I looked up and saw him for the first time. It was the same man whose question had dissolved me into tears just months before.

"I woke up this morning," the neighbour continued. "I was able to dress myself and eat some breakfast. My wife and children and grandchildren are all well."

He wasn't done. He patted Kinu's head. Kinu licked his hand. I resigned myself to listening.

"And here I stand now, in front of my own house, talking to my neighbour and her nice dog in a great neighbourhood. I live in a great country."

He still wasn't done.

"I am a blessed man."

He stopped then, and I stood speechless, suddenly taken aback by the soulful words. They sounded like a hymn of praise to God and to life. And like a benediction.

"Thank you," I said at last.

As Kinu and I walked away, I decided to start counting my blessings, particularly on those long awful nights of pain. And I did, that very night.

First, I gave thanks for my loved ones. My husband. My daughters and son-in-law. My sisters and brother. My mother-in-law. My aunts and uncles and cousins and nieces and nephews. For friends and neighbours.

Then, for the air I breathed. For precious sleep, whenever it came. For a house to live in, a garden to look at, for my doctors and therapists, for people who cared. And for a pet dog, who, on some days, almost seemed wise.

As I fell asleep that first night after giving thanks, I heard my mother's voice, softly singing the words from an old hymn:

Count your blessings, count them one by one,
Count your blessings, count them every one ...

Chapter Forty-eight

Retreat

I was in a cantankerous mood, and the closer we got to my destination in north Toronto, the more cantankerous I became.

"It's not too late to turn around," I urged Hamlin. "Normal people have a change of heart all the time. And I am feeling very normal right now."

"I think you're going to love it!" he declared, in the manner of one who can afford to give assurance since he's not the one heading for the gallows.

"It" was a Lenten retreat in a convent of Anglican nuns. Lent is traditionally a time to give up something of the world, and giving up a weekend in February didn't seem like much at the time. Hamlin and I also both felt that I needed to get out of the house, to be among other people.

The message from our retreat planner had promised "lots of time for quiet, rest, walks, reading ..." Except now that my bags were packed and the car was just minutes from the convent, I suddenly realized what I had signed up for. Two days without family, friends, or any of the usual distractions of telephone, television, radio, or even the busy-ness of housework. Two days with a bunch of women who wore strange costumes and lived apart from the world.

Nuns were among the last people I'd normally choose as weekend mates. As a child, I had heard various whispered stories about nuns: that they considered themselves brides of Christ – as weird a concept as a kid could imagine; that each had a shaved head; that if you ever tried to lift up the head-covering of a nun to find out if this was true, you would be struck blind *and* mute. I had never had any reason to prove or disprove those stories. As I neared the convent, I realized that I was off to spend a weekend with people whose presence still made me nervous, even as an adult.

But that wasn't all. I continued to frown at the letter that was sitting open on my lap. "... In order to keep the spirit of the Retreat, conversations should be held outdoors ... Meals are eaten in silence."

I sat back in my car seat and folded my arms across my chest. Two days in which no one would talk to me and I would talk to no one, unless I chose to go outside in the middle of winter and drag someone out with me. The letter had clearly said, "Please don't hesitate to contact me if you have any questions or concerns." But I had been too preoccupied to ask questions or to even contemplate what I had signed up for, and now it was too late.

You'd think, after all the time I'd spent in silence lately, the countless hours in which my only companions were an old house and a dog, I'd be used to silence. But that silence was in my own house, and, though it often made me miserable, to some extent it was on my own terms. This weekend was going to be in someone else's home and entirely on other people's terms.

Nuns.

"St. John's Convent, the Mother House of the Sisterhood of St. John the Divine, is located ... north of

Finch between Yonge and Bayview. The Convent is easily accessible from Highway 401."

A long curving drive took us from the entrance gates to the convent's guest house.

I interrupted my own querulous imaginings to ask no one in particular, "And who calls himself 'John the Divine'? The height of vanity, wouldn't you say? I mean, if you were a guy named John, would you really refer to yourself as 'the Divine'?"

Hamlin wisely kept silent against my barrage of babble, recognizing it as a subterfuge for fear. Concerned that I would still change my mind, he wished me a quick farewell at the door, barely pecked my cheek, and escaped. I gritted my teeth and prepared for the worst.

The reception room was surprisingly warm and comfortably furnished with elegant sofas and chairs. The tall, middle-aged nun who greeted me was polite but uttered only a few words, spoken very quietly. I followed her down the hall.

She stopped in front of a small sliver of a room, motioned to it, and told me that I would be staying in Julian of Norwich, a room dedicated to an English mystic of that name.

"And what was her claim to fame?" I asked.

"She got herself walled up into a tiny room behind a church – where she spent the rest of her life silently writing and talking to God."

A grim prophecy about this weekend, I thought. My feet refused to take another step. I turned around to face the nun, but for the second time within minutes, another person had taken off before I could change my mind. I was left alone to face my silent cubicle and myself.

A shock of pain radiated from my lower back right down to my foot, pain so bad that I reached for my handbag. But I had left the emergency painkillers at home, thinking I'd try to meditate and visualize my way through the pain this weekend.

Being here is not a good idea, I thought again as I looked at the room. Julian of Norwich was lit by a single window.

"A slight improvement on being walled in," I muttered, placing my bag on the solitary chair.

Without the window, the room would have been a cell. Everything about it was small, even humble. Julian of Norwich was outfitted with a small chest of drawers, chair, bedside table, and a twin-sized bed. Just inside the doorway was a small sink. Plain white cotton sheets and an aging but sturdy blanket had been placed on the unmade bed. Well, it was something to do until I met with the rest of my group, I thought.

～

"All are welcome in this sacred space, offering gentle hospitality, comfortable accommodation, retreats and spiritual direction in an atmosphere of transformative stillness." So read the SSJD brochure.

The Sisterhood of St. John the Divine was founded nearly 130 years ago, said the brochure. Each nun takes a vow of poverty, chastity, and obedience. The women live a monastic life in which they own all things "in common" and follow a daily rhythm of prayer, meditation, work, and rest. The nuns offer "monastic hospitality" to their visitors, based on the belief that each person who comes to their door is a representation of God.

～

The Mother House convent, with its guest house and famous labyrinth, sat on acres of grass and woods in the north end of Toronto. Some guests came here to walk the labyrinth, an inner journey represented by a physical one.

I was not ready to walk that distance, but even if I had been, this was a freezing February weekend: I couldn't even discern the outlines of the labyrinth as I stared out a window. Any journeying would have to take place in the interior landscape. Julian of Norwich came to mind, and I grimaced as I turned away from the wintry scene outside.

~

I smiled as I recognized members of the retreat group to which I would belong this weekend, and they happily returned my smile, but no one spoke. Floating by us were the Sisters of St. John, and none of us wanted to flout their house rules. They wore bright blue robes, a big improvement on the scary black habits of the nuns from my childhood. But uniforms have a way of evening out difference; the people wearing them tend to all look alike. In their long robes, these nuns even seemed to move in rhythm.

I studiously searched for signs of individuality among them. At first, I could discern only the very obvious: that one over there is very tall; that one is short; that one is round; that one is angular; that one is blonde, that one has beautiful dark hair; that one looks like a Dresden doll; that one over there looks like she could easily tackle you in a game of football.

As one Sister passed me in the hallway on the way to supper, I noticed her name tag, and it briefly warmed my heart: her name was Louise. As we lined up to enter the dining room, picked up our napkins (mine was in the wooden cubby hole labelled "Julian of Norwich"), and took our seats, I realized I was seated directly across from her. I smiled, wanting, but not daring, to say, "You have the same name as my mother." She smiled back.

We stood to give thanks for our meal, and, table by table, headed to the buffet, which was laden with an abundance of comfort food: lasagna, homemade bread, cheeses, jams and jellies, and vegetables and fruit. Back at our long refectory table, I ate the delicious food, alone with my thoughts in the midst of a group: solitude in the middle of a multitude. But enforced silence, while sitting in severe pain across from a woman who bore my mother's name, was suffocating. I needed a distraction.

I grabbed the slender book I had quickly borrowed from the library near my room and opened it to read in silence. But Sister Louise reacted immediately.

"You may read after eating," she said. "We encourage you to enjoy the meal."

I was suddenly six years old again, sneaking a book to the dining table and being corrected by my mother.

Incarnation of God or not, I realized that I had just committed my first act of gracelessness. As I looked into a face that was both friendly and firm, it occurred to me that if God himself had been sitting across from her and had committed the same faux pas, Sister Louise would have corrected him in the same way.

"Well, at least someone spoke," I said to console myself, as I left after finishing my meal.

Back in Julian of Norwich, the room seemed even smaller. It was now evening, and without the daylight there was no view to the exterior. I had spent years feeling trapped in a large old house. But this – this wasn't even a room.

"Julian," I said, feeling sad and and remembering this woman's choice to lock herself up in a tiny cell, "What on earth were you thinking?"

Julian didn't answer. Instead, my mother's voice spoke loudly and clearly inside my head.

"God never gives us more than we can handle," she reminded me.

"Oh yes, he does," I replied. "I'm sorry, Mama, but sometimes he does."

The thought triggered sudden introspection. Julian, following her enormous faith in God, chose to be locked up in a cell, and there she stayed, seemingly content. I, meanwhile, had been feeling trapped in a house. Was it the size of her faith that allowed her to handle self-inflicted imprisonment in a tiny space? And, injuries aside, is it the lack of my own faith that makes me feel unbearably trapped in a relatively large old house?

～

It was time for Evensong, a short service of contemplation and readings, held in the convent chapel at the end of the day. I was taken aback by the simple beauty of this modern space. The anteroom sported plump, comfortable armchairs and a fireplace. The sanctuary had large windows; unpretentious wooden chairs instead of pews; light-coloured wooden furniture.

I thought of Wordsworth's words:

It is a beauteous evening, calm and free
The holy time is quiet as a nun, breathless with adoration
The broad sun is sinking down in its tranquility ...

A simple altar stood at one end of the room, a large font at the other, with a long space in the middle. Banks of chairs faced each other across this space, and the sisters were seated in the front rows of both sides, leaving plenty of room for their guests.

The spare simplicity of the service matched its environment: it was a responsive program with long moments for contemplation. I opened my mouth to whisper the written response, but given this rare chance to speak, my voice sounded inappropriately loud.

I contemplated the faces of the Sisters and their chosen lifestyle. The silence is bad enough, I thought, but how does anyone pray for at least two hours a day? I can barely get a prayer to last two minutes, and some nights, just before drifting off to sleep, I shortcut even that. I tell God – the God of my mother, but the God that I still only half believe in: "Well, God, you know all things. So you already know what I would like to pray for. Amen."

But there wasn't much to be learned from simple scrutiny of the nuns' faces as we sat in the chapel. In here, the women simply read, said short prayers, and contemplated. None of them seemed "breathless with adoration," which I found to be a great relief.

Still, as I returned to my room, a phrase that the nuns and their guests repeated was still sounding in my head: "... Renew a right spirit within me." I found myself repeating it silently.

As I entered the tiny room, Julian of Norwich still felt claustrophobic but not quite as scary as before. I was not desperate enough to escape – just yet. Perhaps I could last another day, I told myself. I suddenly wanted to call my husband, to tell him I had survived so far. But there was no phone, of course, and it didn't occur to me till the morning that I could have used my cell phone.

Instead, I flipped open the book about Julian of Norwich that I'd brought with me from the library.

Julian of Norwich, the book said, was a philosopher and mystic who lived from 1342 to 1413. She became famous for the words she wrote after her "conversations with God." Some were complex ideas about moral decisions; others were her conclusions after asking God a question and not receiving a direct reply. Perhaps the most famous is her reassurance that whatever God does is done in love and that "all shall be well, and all shall be well, and all manner of thing shall be well."

I read for an hour and went to sleep under the fresh sheets and old blanket. I slept surprisingly well.

~

When I sneaked a call to Hamlin the next morning, his greeting was, "Want me to come and bust you out of there?"

"No," I replied, in a whisper. "I'm trying my best to hang in. No promises, mind you. Keep your cell phone on! What are you doing?"

"You'd be surprised how quiet it was here last night," he said, "just Kinu and me, a couple of guys hanging out by the fireplace, with a glass of port and watching TV."

I smiled at the image of Kinu hoisting a glass of port.

"There's no one to ask us any questions," Hamlin teased. "It's really nice and quiet, like a silent retreat."

I groaned out loud, but grinned into the phone.

In the throng of people at the convent this weekend, I started picking out the few nuns whose faces I recognized. Finally the moment came where our retreat group headed into a meeting room for our sole opportunity for a seminar.

Sister Sue, the plain-talking retreat leader, won my respect the first time she talked about the Book of Psalms, that famous collection of songs to God from writers living in pastoral times thousands of years ago. The psalms are prayers of praise, supplication, lamentation — along with fervent pleas for God to strike down the writer's enemies. In some cases, it appeared, a simple smiting was too good for those who had wronged the psalmist; God is asked to also commit great violence against them, their families, their fields, and even their livestock. It is this bloodlust that made me somewhat skeptical of the Bible.

Perhaps Sister Sue sensed that there was a skeptic in the room, because she got right down to business, addressing what she called "the naughty bits" of the psalms. With intelligence, warmth, and humour, she guided us through a discussion about the relevance of these ancient writings to our modern lives, including those times when people have hurt us, and we'd like nothing better than for God to smite them, or those times when we feel God himself has let us down.

Sister Sue also answered the question I wanted to ask: Why on earth would a modern, intelligent woman give up her profession, her own dwelling, and all her worldly goods to make her home in a convent?

Different women take different journeys, she said. Hers came from a promise to God while in a ho-hum career as a college professor: if she was in the same career situation by a certain time, she had told God, she would dedicate her life to his service. And so she did.

The single figure who completely bowled me over that weekend was Sister Thelma-Anne, an elderly nun perhaps eighty years old. As she took her seat in the chapel, I saw that her small body was painfully misaligned and stooped over to one side from Parkinson's disease. She shuffled over to the organ, sat, and started to play.

The sacred music that broke forth was achingly beautiful. My throat tightened up as the music soared from the pipes on the walls far above Sister Thelma-Anne's body. Her face held my attention throughout, a striking accompaniment to the magnificent music: it was completely radiant, lit from within by serenity and joy.

Perhaps it was this Sister's example that got to me, because from somewhere came the thought that if this woman can survive the affliction of her disease, show up on time for the service, and play the organ so powerfully, then surely I could survive this weekend without complaining.

~

The last time I had felt truly trapped in a religious community – in the small, over-religious country village of my adolescence – books had been my lifeline to a world beyond. Perhaps books would also help me this time, to keep my pledge of not complaining.

I made my way to the library down the hall. This time, I looked around. The room was comfortably furnished with soft upholstered chairs, a sofa, and shaded lamps, but the contents that counted most for me were the ones that could be read: the books.

When the weekend was over, I left the convent with no intention of returning. I had survived the weekend, but I didn't want to push my luck.

Chapter Forty-nine

St. Martin's Day

"Ancora imparo," said the great Michelangelo when he was all of eighty-seven. "I am still learning."

Around the bend to the right of our house, just a few houses away, lived Vito, the neighbour who had spoken so eloquently about his life's blessings. He appeared to be in his late sixties. He wore large, dark-rimmed glasses and a cap that covered a full head of dark hair just turning grey.

I now walked Kinu once or twice a week, and every time we passed Vito's house, Kinu slowed down long enough for Vito to notice and join us for a chat. It was still mostly a one-sided chat, but Vito seemed to think it was worth his time. I, meanwhile, was grateful that he never mentioned the obvious. He never asked about my injuries and never asked how I was coping.

Vito spoke, and I listened. He was deeply knowledgeable about history, wine, gardening, and other things, and it was clear that he loved language. He used it formally, elegantly; his choice of words was especially impressive, since English was his third language.

I told him once that he spoke like a professor of English. He stared at me, shocked either because I'd mistaken him for a professor or because I had actually spoken in a sentence.

"No. Not me," he finally answered. "I am far less. I am an ordinary labourer."

He said the words almost wistfully, as if he would have really liked to be a professor of English but would never admit it.

References to history peppered his remarks, along with Italian proverbs.

One autumn, during winemaking season, I asked, "Vito, when will the grape juice turn into wine?"

Everyone else I knew would have said, "Oh, around mid-November or so."

Not Vito.

"Di San Martino ogni mosto e vino," he replied and waited for me to figure it out. Vito knew that I could still speak some Italian. But he'd also figured out that on some days my mind was so groggy, I could barely speak English.

So he translated. "On St. Martin's Day, the must turns to wine."

One day I asked another question: "Why are so many villages and towns in Italy named San Vito?"

I remembered this because I had worked often in Italy in the decade before the accident.

"In the year 303, when Christians were still being killed because of their faith ..." Vito began.

A couple minutes later I found out that the towns were named in honour of the Christian martyr Saint Vitus, patron saint of entertainers and epileptics.

Another time, he casually mentioned that his first name was meant to be the same as his father's.

"So what happened?"

"That beautiful asshole named Mussolini passed a law in 1940, the very year I was born, that no son could have the same name as his father ..."

Vito shrugged eloquently.

I had heard the fascist Italian wartime leader described

in many different ways, but never before as a beautiful rectum.

When he was still a teen, Vito and his father escaped the poverty of southern Italy and went to work on farms in France. It meant an abrupt end to his formal schooling and the start of his learning to speak French. The family came to Ontario, Canada, next, so Vito had to learn yet another language, English.

All the while, he told me once, he read books. First in Italian, then in French, then in English, and finally, any of the above. And because he lacked formal education, he never stopped learning.

He and his wife Loretta spent a lot of time in their large, Italian-style kitchen. The room was crammed full of books, particularly dictionaries.

Loretta told me that she had ordered Vito to never bring another book into the house. Already, the books took up way too much space in her kitchen, she said. But of course, Vito simply ignored the order.

The pages of his thick dictionaries were marked with dozens of bits of paper. Whenever Vito came across a new word, he looked it up in either the English-Italian, Italian-English, or French-Italian dictionary. And then marked it.

"He has a system with those books," Loretta said, rolling her eyes. "But only he understands it."

One day, out of the blue, Vito confessed that for years he had dreamed of buying the farmhouse I now lived in. Mostly, he had wanted the land, to plant his own vines, make his own wine, and grow a lot of vegetables. But by the time it came up for sale, he and Loretta had decided they were too old to move.

"I had big plans for that place," he said, shaking his head as if to clear it of regret. "I would have had a huge garden. *A huge garden.*"

A few days later, Vito came to visit our house. He was entirely unimpressed by what we'd done with the garden.

"All this land – and you have no garden!" he muttered.

"But I do have a garden." I pointed to the flowerbeds. "There it is!"

Sizing up the situation, Hamlin invited Vito to see his beloved vegetable patch instead.

Vito muttered something in Italian. Then French. Then English.

"You have all this land – and no garden."

He shook his head. It was obvious that he thought we were barbarians. With this much land, how could decent people not fill it with grapevines and vegetables?

I pleaded for understanding. "Vito, I can't garden anymore. And Hamlin has his hands full since I had the accident."

But Vito's disappointment had overwhelmed him. He left, still shaking his head.

"Think he'll ever forgive us?" I asked Hamlin.

"I'm not sure," he said. "But I know this much: I'm expanding the vegetable garden in the fall."

~

Fall arrived, and before we knew it, the maple leaves had turned gold and scarlet and fallen onto the lawns and sidewalks, creating a glorious mess. For years, this was my favourite season. But although we had lived in this neighbourhood for several years, this was the first time I really noticed how active it became in the fall.

The whole neighbourhood seemed to be painting, planting, and – most popular of all – preserving. It was the season for turning grapes into wine, tomatoes into sauce, apples and mint into jelly.

Across the street, in his garage, a neighbour was preparing meats for curing. Big chunks that will hang from a long wooden stick in his cold room for months until they're fully cured. Then they're called pancetta, capicola, prosciutto.

A few doors down, family members of all ages gathered in their garage to split enormous sweet red peppers in two, remove the seeds and stems, coat the glistening red chunks with olive oil, and roast them on the barbecue. The whole process makes the peppers sweeter when they're eaten weeks and months later.

Farther down the street, Paddy and Jacquie were preparing their garden for the fall. This couple had been the first to welcome us to the neighbourhood. Every so often they dropped in, bringing Jamaican codfish fritters, mangoes, and words of encouragement. One day, recently, I surprised them with a jar of apple jelly, which I made myself with apples from the two trees in our garden.

~

"Make jelly," therapist Sarah advised me one day.

I had just revealed that making jelly was one of the few times when I could empty my mind of worries about the future. Although a very simple activity to most people who do it, making jelly required me to focus my entire being on the apples as I cut them up, on the measured quantities of apple juice and sugar that I mixed into the large pot, on the bubbling liquid that I stirred and watched diligently to prevent it from boiling over.

~

Vito's place around the corner was Operation Central. Dozens of empty flat wooden crates were neatly piled up on one side of his driveway. The garage door was rolled up. For the next two weeks, Vito would be a vintner like his father and grandfather before him. He would crush the grapes, store the juice (the must) in tall, thick, blue plastic containers, and pour the liquid into oak barrels to ferment.

I stopped to check on his progress.

"I don't remember when the wine will be ready," I said.

Vito turned, gave me a warm, welcoming smile, and played along with me: "Di San Martino ogni mosto e vino." On the feast day of St. Martin ... when the must turns to wine.

In November, after St. Martin's Day, Vito brought us a large bottle of merlot. He toured the outlines of the expanded garden bed, nodding approvingly. Minutes before, I had warned Vito that only positive criticism would be tolerated.

"OK," he agreed, nodding. "I'll give only *critica positiva.*"

Vito was true to his word. He even sounded genuine when he gave Hamlin the good news.

Hamlin's smile spread right across his face.

Chapter Fifty

All Shall Be Well

I had left the Sisters of St. John the Divine with absolutely no intention of returning. But I did, triggered by two things.

The first was a comment by Hamlin: "You don't realize it, but when you go on retreat, it's a retreat for me, as well – from you!"

He was teasing – I thought – but what he said made sense. For years I had been stuck inside the house, rarely venturing out. The business trips, the occasional visits to my girlfriends who lived out of town – those were now all things of the past.

The second was my discovery, days after leaving the convent the year before, that I had unintentionally removed two of the nuns' books. Since I removed them in error, you might have expected me to return them right away, penitent for my actions. But I decided to read them instead. One book was written by an author who, like me, wants to believe in God but struggles with her lack of steady faith.

Weeks later, I decided to call the Sisters, confess, and then return the books. But every time I picked up the phone to call them, I was struck by the same question.

How do you tell the nuns that you inadvertently stole their books, and that, having discovered your crime, you decided to go ahead and enjoy the stolen goods anyway? The only solution I could think of was to return the books quietly. And the only way I knew of to get into the nuns' library was to show up as a guest. I booked my space in the next retreat.

The following February, on another wintry Canadian day, we turned into the driveway of the convent. I shared with my husband my clever plan to slip into the library and put the books back on the shelf when no one was looking. For some reason, he found this very funny. Before I knew it, we were both howling with laughter.

As we got closer to the entrance of the guest house, however, I got cold feet again. When the nun opened the door, I became immediately convinced that she had X-ray vision and had seen the books in my luggage.

I plodded timidly behind her up the elevator and down the hallway, passing several guest rooms: St. Anne, St. Catherine, and others. She suddenly stopped at a familiar doorway and waited for me there. It was Julian of Norwich.

"Hello, Julian!" I called out in silent greeting. "Long time no see."

I reached into my bag for the books, tucked them under my jacket, and scooted off to the library at the end of the hall.

~

"Our real blessings often appear to us in the shape of pains, losses, and disappointments," Joseph Addison wisely noted. "But let us have patience and we shall soon see them in their proper figures."

A retreat with the Sisters of St. John the Divine became a kind of once-a-year, home-away-from-home visit. By my third visit, I knew what to expect. The silence was no longer frightening and was even welcome.

I never brought painkillers with me, choosing instead to practice meditation, visualization, yoga, and other skills the therapists at the rehabilitation hospital had taught me. And when all these things failed, I prayed. I counted my blessings, one by one.

There were no miracle cures at these retreats, but I did notice that in the stillness of the convent, without the daily clutter of talk and distractions, a fresh new idea would make its way through the haze of pain, and issues that seemed monumental were reduced to their proper size.

Each time I arrived, the nuns assigned me to Julian of Norwich, as if willing me to understand one of her most famous messages: "He said not: thou shalt not be troubled, thou shalt not be tempted, thou shalt not be distressed; He said: thou shalt not be overcome."

On this third visit, when my friend Judy, a first-timer, got an attack of fright over the reality of being in a silent convent, I empathized with her immediately.

"At this stage," she whispered furtively, "I'd be grateful if someone would cough, or even sneeze. I feel like busting out and heading to the nearest mall, just to hear people talk!"

I hugged her and laughed quietly. I whispered that there were good things to look forward to: great food, a comfortable library, time for peaceful meditation, time with a group of women whose individual personalities, hospitality, and sense of community go a far way to creating an environment of peace and harmony. There was also beautiful music, and, with luck, Sister Thelma-Anne would play the organ again.

All shall be well, and all shall be well, and all manner of thing shall be well.

Chapter Fifty-one

New Wine

Through the mudroom window, I watched Hamlin stroll, just a little unsteady, up the path to our side door, Kinu walking alongside him. Something was definitely wrong. Maybe he had hurt his foot.

I opened the door for them, just in case.

"Are you aware that you're listing to the right?" I asked.

A foolish grin spread across my husband's face.

"With good reason!" he said. "Vito and the others ... the vintners of the neighbourhood ... have designated me their official wine taster."

He rolled his eyes and shrugged helplessly.

"Everyone claims they just want what they call 'an outside opinion' from me," he said. "But really, they all want me to say their wine is the best. Kinu and I go down the street for a walk, and before I know it, someone is dragging me onto their verandah for a tasting."

He laughed. "You want to know something? It's driving me to drink!"

I laughed with him. Hamlin is a man who knows his wines but rarely drinks. Until this day, I had never seen him even slightly sauced.

"Don't buy the house, buy the neighbourhood," says a Russian proverb. We had bought a house, and now we had finally become part of the neighbourhood. At first, this was undoubtedly thanks to Kinu, who made friends wherever he went. But it was also because of Hamlin's kindness. When a neighbour's lawnmower broke down, he lent his. When another neighbour took ill during the winter, Hamlin crossed the road with his snowblower and cleared his driveway. When a couple went off on a cruise, Hamlin collected their mail for them.

The neighbours often repaid his kindness in food. Andrew, originally from Malaysia, sometimes showed up at our front door with freshly cooked, spicy food, while George and Kiki brought plates of roast lamb or Greek pastries. Someone else brought us jars of homemade tomato sauce. Matthew and Suzi reaped Asian greens from their garden and stuffed them in a big plastic bag, which they passed over the back fence. Diane brought us raspberry jam and encouragement. And of course, there was always plenty of homemade wine. And impromptu wine tastings.

There was no doubt about it. Home wasn't just a family's house and garden. Home was also one's neighbourhood. I had missed that truth for most of the time we'd lived here, but now I understood it, loud and clear.

"So, exactly how much wine did they make you drink today?" I asked Hamlin.

"Not too sure. But these guys make strong wine. *Really* strong wine ..." He squinted, forehead furrowed, then gave up trying to calculate the amount. Right now, he needed to know a different truth.

"Was I really listing to the right?"

"Yes, you and Kinu both. Was he drinking, too?"

But we both knew what was wrong with Kinu. The

malady that affects large-breed dogs, hip displacement, had slowed him right down. Our beloved pet, whom we adopted as a young pup twelve years before, when we lived in the blue house, was now approaching the end of his natural life. Kinu was getting old, and, despite his boundlessly happy nature, his body was letting him down.

Chapter Fifty-two

Strength from the Past

Hamlin was determined that our farmhouse with the unusual apple trees would be our permanent home. We knew what it was like to give up a house and property we loved because it was the right thing to do. We had done this twice before. Now, I watched him work harder, making up for my inability to work steadily.

"You just focus on getting better," he often told me. "Don't think about anything else."

Hamlin had also been determined to find the stories I had written over more than twenty years, believing they would help me find the strength I needed to face my uncertain future.

He roamed from room to room and moved things around. He seemed to be tearing the house apart. Finally, with a huge smile across his face, he walked into the bedroom, waving some papers in the air. He had found the first of my stories.

Over the course of a year, he found more of them, some in the basement, in old computers; some in the garage, in dusty old boxes; some at the back of closets where they had been placed and forgotten when we moved in.

I had written the stories across twenty-five years,

subconsciously marking the chapters of my life. Hamlin found them, printed them out, or dusted them off, and handed them to me, one by one.

It would take him nearly a year to find them – nearly sixty stories in all – and I would read every one of them, snorting with disbelief, weeping, or laughing out loud.

The houses and places where I had lived came to vivid life in the stories. So did the people. But I hardly recognized myself in these stories: the six-year old daredevil; the stubborn child of ten who insisted on fighting her way through the throngs of giants at the grand market on a Saturday; the teenager who left her homeland on two weeks' notice; the young woman who went to school during the day and worked at night, year after year.

The mother whose children laughed out loud when her first attempts at making cookies for the bake sale at school turned out disastrously; the same mother who fought like a bear to help her children succeed in school and in life; the wife who fiercely believed in her husband, encouraging him each step of the way; the daughter who tried to support her parents.

Then there was the leader who faced down one challenge after another and won national awards and international acclaim for outstanding achievement.

Who was this woman?

Who was this woman who had hoisted heavy rocks to build a long stone wall, who dug into untamed soil to build garden beds, who never saw a challenge she didn't think she could overcome?

Even the thought of her exhausted me.

Who was this woman, and where had she gone? Since the accident, she had quit leading the huge projects, quit public speaking, quit public life. But was she still a writer, a gardener, a daughter, a mother, a wife? And if not, what then? And why had she always kept moving? Why had she never stood still long enough in any one place? What had she been searching for?

~

Weeks after finding the first set of stories, Hamlin encouraged me to send one to the Canadian art and design magazine *Arabella*. When the editor asked if I had any images to accompany it, Hamlin, an avid photographer, went and took the photos himself and sent them off. The editor also asked me for more of the stories.

Every time a new issue of the magazine came out, we searched for my story and his photos like children opening a Christmas present.

~

I often returned to the stories, trying to learn something useful for my present circumstances.

I had enjoyed a blessed life, filled with adventure, challenges, abundant success. But I had not done it alone. Many people had come into my life when needed, people who helped me along the way.

My relatives, my first role models: these people were fighters, people whose courage and resilience had fuelled my own success. From these women and men, I'd learned how to overcome challenges, how to be strong.

"What doesn't kill you makes you strong," my mother used to say. And I had worked hard at being strong, determined that no challenge would ever be allowed to do me in.

And then came the accident. As if to prove that no one is invincible, it left my body weak and damaged, my mind worn down from injury, pain, and psychological trauma. I had finally prayed for death to come.

"There are none so blind as those who will not see," my mother used to tell me when I'd walked right past a truth that was staring me in the face.

My role models had been strong warriors, and I had emulated them. But I had missed the one thing that might have helped me through these tough times: the times when they felt too weak to carry on, the times when the adversity they faced seemed about to do them in. They must have felt all these things along the way, but I hadn't given it much thought.

"Those were the times they stopped and asked for help," my eldest sister, Yvonne, said when I telephoned her in Texas. "From God, from relatives and friends, from the church, and from the village around them."

Around me now, a village had been quietly forming. A village marked, not by geography, but by citizens determined to see me through this time of trial.

My husband, daughters and son-in-law, siblings, mother-in-law. My uncle Gerald in London, England, my great-aunt Rose in New Jersey.

Our friends at the little village church to which we returned, despite having moved away.

The unexpected visitors, children of the old farmhouse, their stories bringing the house – and me – to life.

Our new neighbours, bearing gifts of food, wine, fruit, and encouragement.

My doctors, therapists, friends.

Not all my old friends. Some simply disappeared, as though melting away, unable or unwilling to stay in touch with a woman who was rarely seen in public, and who, on her worst days, made no sense at all. But other friends stood by me, becoming more precious as time went by.

I had always been the one to offer help but had never really been comfortable asking for it. Slowly, I began to learn how to ask.

Family gatherings were now truly a communal affair, not just in the eating and drinking and laughter, but in the cooking and cleaning that accompany them. Relatives and friends no longer asked if they could help. They called to tell me what they were going to do, what they were going to bring. I was thankful.

We had a dishwasher, and on such occasions it was put to good use. But when the conversation or the sitting wore me out, I headed to the kitchen sink and started washing dishes, enjoying the feeling of being useful, of the warm soapy water on my hands, of the chance to contemplate.

These were sacred moments. There were days when I was sure that God was to be found in the dirty dishes, not the clean ones. When I argued with God over the dirty dishes, it was a friendly argument. And when I gave thanks for the many blessings of my life, it was with heartfelt gratitude.

Gradually, the old house also became a friend. We had spent so much time alone together that I had come to know both its silence and its sounds, the way it looked when the sun poured through its many windows, and the way it felt late at night when everyone else slumbered in its soft silence.

Nikisha had taken to showing up for tea and chat or to take me out of the house for lunch. I would have declined a year earlier, especially if the pain was too great. Now I remembered my mother's motto: "When your children invite you out, drop everything else and go." It sometimes meant swiftly swallowing an emergency painkiller before leaving the house.

Lauren completed her studies, got a job that she loved, and found herself a new apartment. She was finally able to cover the rent without needing to split costs with a roommate and was glad to have her own space. It was a bright, comfortable place. It was a joy to watch her turn the apartment into a home and to see her come into her own.

Lauren still came home for the occasional weekend.

Sometimes, when she visited, she and I snuggled up in bed, dogs at our feet, three pillows behind my back, watching a movie on her laptop. *The Secret Garden. Remember the Titans.* Or episodes from *Downton Abbey*, the British TV series.

Once in a while, at the end of a long, tiring day at work, she would call, complaining about having to take care of the two dogs she had adopted. I listened patiently, knowing how much she loved Julius and Dawson, knowing she just needed to vent.

"I feel like a single mother of two dogs!" she said. "Was it this tough for you and Dad, raising two kids?"

"A little bit tougher, but definitely worth it."

She laughed and I could feel her stress diminishing.

Our relationship had changed since the day our family met with my therapist, Sarah, a woman experienced in dealing with people who suffer from chronic pain, head injuries, and post-traumatic stress. Still unable to talk about the toughest issues, I had to leave the room.

For some strange reason, Sarah thought I was courageous. The first time she said this, I asked her what she was smoking. The second time she said it was to my family, after I had left the room. Her words made everyone, including the therapist herself, cry.

Whatever happened in that room must have helped my family. My children seemed a bit more knowledgeable and a bit more patient with me ever since.

What Remains

It's early springtime, but winter refuses to leave gracefully. The two seasons are fighting it out. The apple trees
sway in the wind, looking for all the world as though about
to keel over, or snap in two. Rain lashes the windowpanes,
the wind keens around the house making sure that we are
aware of its mighty presence.

Hamlin and I gaze at the part of the garden where we
know we will soon see the fig tree again. After we moved
to the farmhouse, and after Hamlin got to know the neighbours better, one of them told him how to keep the tree
alive over the winter. Come fall, he said, you dig a trough
in the garden bed and bury the tree in it, then cover it
with about eighteen inches of garden soil and leaves.

Hamlin had to fight back disbelief that first time.
He buried the tree and worried about it throughout the
winter. But sure enough, when he dug it up in the spring,
not only was it very much alive, but it had pale green
leaves, and baby figs were forming.

I consider the old apple trees. One is large and strong
and vigorous, the other less so, having lost one of its two
largest limbs twenty years ago. Almost as old as the house,
these trees are a small miracle. They bear thousands of

fruit one year, resting the next. In the year of abundance, the trees are covered with light pink blossoms for nearly two weeks in May. The trees' fruit tastes slightly different, but both still produce.

I consider the old farmhouse. The many times and humans it has survived, the daily sounds of living it has heard ... the yells and shouts, the murmur of familial conversations, the small thuds of children's feet racing across its floors, the sudden laughter, the soft tears of sorrow, the final goodbyes. Words of love, anguish, prayer.

Edith Wharton, the American author, wrote "... a woman's nature is like a great house full of rooms: here is the hall through which everyone passes going in and out; the drawing room where one receives formal visits, the sitting room where members of the family come and go as they wish, but beyond that, far beyond, there are other rooms, the handles of which are never turned ..."

So much good remains in my life. So much to love. So much to find strength in. Rooms not yet entered, handles not yet turned.

The wind continues to flay the old house. A loose shutter rattles against an exterior wall. But the house stands firm, as it and the apple trees have done for more than a century.

~

I sit alone in the corner of a bedroom, reading one poem, then another. The first is Wordsworth's poem of consolation over the loss, to urban development, of the meadows and fields that he played in as a small child.

The radiance which was once so bright
Is now forever taken from my sight
Though nothing can bring back the hour of splendour in
the grass

Of glory in the flower
We will grieve not
Rather, find strength in what remains behind.

Find strength in what remains behind. I read the last line aloud. Twice. The first time I read it to our farmhouse with its lost fields. The second time, to myself.

The second poem is by Derek Walcott. Like me, he is a child of the Caribbean, but I had never heard of this poem until the therapists at the rehabilitation hospital in Toronto read it to me. These people have worked hard to put me back together, body and soul, these past two years. They have patiently chipped away at my anger and despair, and now are trying to rub smooth the jagged edges that remain. Reading this poem is part of the process.

The time will come
When, with elation,
you will greet yourself arriving
at your own door, in your own mirror,
and each will smile at the other's welcome
and say, sit here. Eat.
You will love again the stranger who was yourself.

Home at Last

I t is a quiet evening in the old farmhouse.

Hamlin sits on the living room sofa, reading a book. Two weekend visitors are curled up at his feet: our daughter Lauren's puppies, Julius Caesar, the little brown dog with the big name, and Dawson, the even smaller white stray that she rescued a year ago.

Dawson slipped into our family and treats our house and grounds as if he's lived here forever. When we miss him, he's likely at the fence, where his white fur makes him almost invisible against the white pickets. He stands on his hind legs, nose and eyes poking through the space between pickets in the fence that surrounds our house. Sooner or later, Julius joins him. There they wait, quiet as mice, until an unsuspecting passerby is right in front of them, separated only by the fence. Then they let out a chorus of fearsome barks. When the person jumps and squeals in fright, Lauren or Hamlin runs to the fence, apologizing profusely to the person, who has already fled.

Sitting in the living room with Hamlin and the dogs, I look through the tall, mullioned windows of the farmhouse, remembering, imagining. Kinu. Our beloved family pet.

If Kinu were here now, he'd probably be running through the snow, poking his head right into it, then pulling it out swiftly and taking off again, his paw prints leaving a snow pattern right around the house. That dog loved the snow so much, we nicknamed him Snow Dragon.

We still miss him. Kinu, the gentle giant whose insistent friendliness to neighbours had helped me break out of my desperate solitude, has been dead for two years now. No other pet has replaced him. We are content to babysit Julius and Dawson, and Nikisha and Tim's two cats, Simon and Jerome, from time to time.

Nikisha and Tim are happily settled in their home, the long, narrow red brick house that Harry found for us all those years ago. In just a few years, they have made more improvements to the house than we did in all our time there. They are steadily making new memories, grafting new ones onto old.

On one wall of our living room is the first painting I ever bought, created by a Jamaican-born artist in the English countryside. My heart warms every time I see it. It reminds me that sometimes we have to take a leap of faith. I had commissioned a painting from an artist who was losing her eyesight, knowing she might not be able to finish it. That artist, Eve, had made the painting and sent it to me in Canada though I hadn't paid her a penny and she had never met me.

On the nearby bookshelf, a silver bowl that once belonged to our old real estate agent Harry sits beside an old book of Canadian history. Harry, who adopted us as family before we quite realized it, bequeathed it to us. He was over ninety years old when he died.

Next to the bowl sits an old history book. Returned to us in an act of repentance, it's a reminder of our country cottage, the old Narnia house so reminiscent of my first childhood home in Jamaica with its stream and trees and small farmhouse. We gave up our magical Ontario cottage to support my parents after my father took critically ill. It was a sacrifice, but one worth making. "People are more important than things," Hamlin said when we sold that home.

We still miss my mother, whose sturdy faith strengthened us in rough times; whose storytelling held us spellbound; whose laughter instantly triggered a good mood.

On the living-room shelves are several photos from Nikisha and Tim's wedding. Some of them show my mother. In one photo, she's wearing a gorgeous bright blue dress. Her eyes are sparkling. Her short silver hair and luminous soft brown skin radiate health, love, hope. I still catch my breath at the sight of it, but always, the image makes me smile.

"Be still, and know that I am God," my mother used to quote from the Bible as I hurried to and fro, waging war against some challenge or trying to save the world. It was hard to be still back then – as a wife, mother, daughter, leader, gardener, writer, and community volunteer. And, back then, I still wasn't even sure that God was God.

Now I am forced to be still in body and mind, to contemplate God, myself, and other mysteries. To consider the presence of the divine in my life. It's been there all along, but I was too busy to connect the dots between the many events that seemed to come from nowhere to change my life or simply improve it.

Along with that discovery has come another: that the commonplace can be a thing of beauty and the mundane, as someone once said, "the edge of glory."

Small things are heard now – heard, seen, and appreciated.

The turn of my husband's key in the lock of the front door; the sound of his steady footfall as he climbs the stairs.

The melody of the large metal wind chimes that hang from the ceiling of our verandah. They produce a music that sounds, incongruously, somewhere between a light, tinkling song and the deep timbre of church bells.

The sight of the three crosses atop the nearby church, lit up at night when the world is still and motionless.

Sometimes I come through a doorway and the old farmhouse astonishes me. I had always known it was beautiful and well built, but had never thought of it as charming. Now I gasp at its soaring, multi-paned windows, the unusual woodwork that trims its ceilings, doorways, windows, and floors. The big, tall, wooden front door with its character-laden transom overhead. The narrow strips of wavy glass on either side of the door.

The charm that Hamlin and I had looked for in our very first house is here in abundance.

The old farmhouse has a feeling of rootedness, permanence, history, all things that I, the immigrant, had searched for over the decades since uprooting myself from Jamaica, perhaps even since leaving the home of my early childhood. Searched for without knowing.

The farmhouse has survived all the changes wrought by the weather, by humans, by time. It's been assaulted by winds from the north and the west, by hurricanes, floods, and storms. And yet, it has retained its spirit. Even without its many acres of farmland, its trees, cows, and horses, even without its farmers, it is still the old farmhouse.

I, too, have been battered and assaulted, my world shaken by huge changes. Gone is my old terrain, the acres of public activity and acclaim, the international travel and presentations to people in different parts of the globe. Other people live in those spaces now.

I've had to pull inward, to occupy the land directly around and inside me. It's a smaller space now, one I am still getting to know, to understand. Rooms to enter, handles to turn.

But I am once again a writer. A writer, a mother, a daughter, a partner, a sister, a neighbour, a friend. And yes, a wife.

And it seems I am finally at home – with myself.

The End

Acknowledgements

It took a village to raise this book!

To the dozens of individuals who encouraged me to keep at it, especially in the tough times: thank you.

Special thanks to my first readers: Lauren Reyes-Grange, Dale Ratcliffe, Jean Gairdner, Carol Shaw, Kamala-Jean Gopie, and Lucia Charlery. You gave frank, yet encouraging, reactions – which I needed.

To Jane, Marion, Les, Pia, Nory, Yvonne, Stephanie, Lee, Louise, Lisa, Bill, Djanka, Beverley, Desrine, Karen, Sarah, Chris, and MaryAnn: thank you for your comments.

Debra and Brian Usher said my stories were good and published some of them in their beautiful magazine, *Arabella*. At CBC Radio, Susan Marjetti, Joan Melanson, and Mark O'Neill said the same and aired an excerpt from the book. I'm grateful for the votes of confidence.

I had terrific editors who helped advance the book to a higher level. Tim Knight, Lesley Marcovich, and Don Bastian: I have been privileged to work with you. I'm very grateful to Don, whose long experience dealing with writers has made him patient, pushy, and empowering all at once.

My thanks to Edward Gajdel, one of Canada's foremost portrait photographers, who took my picture for this book.

My doctors and therapists and my church have helped me keep going through very challenging times. Special thanks to Dr. Rosalie Hooks, Dr. Veronica Kekozs, therapist Sarah Johnson, and the therapists in the Pain Management Centre at Toronto Rehabilitation. Much gratitude to Claire, David, and many others at St. Thomas' Anglican Church in Brooklin, Ontario.

Most of all, I thank my husband, Hamlin, daughters Nikisha and Lauren, and son-in-law Tim; my siblings Yvonne, Pat, Jackie, and Michael, whose own memories of our childhood homes were invaluable for fact-checking and detail; and the other marvellous storytellers in my family, including my mother Louise, mother-in-law Merle, cousins Ken, Beverly, Norma, George, and Lois, uncles Gerald, Eddie, and Jack, aunt Icilda, and my grandmother Artress, great-aunt Rose, and great-grandmother Eliza.

Discussion Guide

A Good Home explores the idea of home from several perspectives – from a first childhood home to finding home in a new land and finally finding the home inside oneself. Underlying these experiences are several sub-themes that also play significant roles in the story.

1   Why is "home" such a powerful force in our lives?
    - What does "home" mean to you?
    - What makes a house become a home?
    - What does it mean, to "go home"? And what does it mean to leave home?

2   At different stages in her life, the narrator lives in very different homes, from a tiny cottage in the Jamaican countryside to an old farmhouse in Ontario, Canada, and even a Frank Lloyd Wright–inspired home situated right next door to a forest.
    - How does each home influence the narrator's life experiences?
    - What kind of relationship does she develop with each home?
    - Do our homes influence our experiences, or do our experiences influence our choice of home?

3 The narrator writes about her natural surroundings as much as she writes about the houses in which she's lived.
- What is the role of nature in this book?
- How does the narrator's affinity for the natural world expand your understanding of her values and her homes?

4 "Home" invariably includes the relationships that unfold in our experience of home, however we define the term.
- How do we experience the key relationships that are connected to "home"?
- How does the narrator negotiate the close relationships in her life, from her relationships with her siblings, mother, father, grandmother, and pet dog to her relationships with her spouse and children?

5 Serendipity and even miracles are also recurring themes in this book: the chance encounter, the unexpected outcome of opening a book, events that seem to owe more to the divine or the ethereal than to logic.
- What is your view of the way these themes are expressed in the book, and does it change your own concepts of serendipity and miracles?

6 Many people associate "home" with peace and stability. But the notion of change and how it affects lives is an underlying theme throughout the book.
- What are some of the ways in which change is portrayed?
- What can others learn about change from the reactions of the narrator and her family, friends, and neighbours in this book?

7   This book is emotionally charged because it deals with big, complex emotions relating to home and relationships: love, loss, healing, and faith.
   - How do the key relationships – including the narrator's relationship with her house, her family, and faith – help her manage the challenges that have been thrown at her?
   - Can a strong connection with "home" help us get through the crises we face at key points in our lives? If so, how?

8   Belief systems are a theme in this book. The narrator talks about both her faith and her lack of faith at certain moments of her life.
   - What beliefs does she have to help see her through the difficult periods?
   - Do you believe in a divine spirit, whether you call that spirit "God" or something else?
   - Does it help to have such spiritual beliefs? Does faith matter?

9   Near the end of the book, the narrator reveals that she is afflicted with chronic pain, post-traumatic stress, and depression as a result of her motor vehicle accident. Each of these illnesses can sometimes lead to suicide.
   - How does she cope with this realization?
   - What insights does she offer to others who are struggling with big issues in their lives?

CPSIA information can be obtained at www.ICGtesting.com
Printed in the USA
LVOW10s1001130813

347647LV00001B/65/P